Intervention:
Anything But My Own Skin

Chad Hepler

Intervention: Anything But My Own Skin

This memoir is a product of the author's recollections and is thus rendered
as a subjective accounting of events that occurred in his life.

Printed in the United States of America

10 9 8 7 6 5 4 3 2 1

ISBN-13: 978-1453673546

This book is dedicated to my parents, Steve and Hollie. Thank you for your undying love and support, and especially for never giving up.

The Departure

The stunning light pierced into my sight, abruptly waking me from a deep sleep. Delirious and groggy, I tried to pull myself together, but nothing made sense. It must have been four in the morning. *What's happening? Am I dreaming? Where am I?* After rubbing my eyes, my vision focused, forming a clear picture of the scene in front of me.

As I sat up in bed, I was engulfed by an overwhelming sense of fear and anxiety. To my immediate right stood both my parents, fully dressed. At the foot of my bed stood a man and a woman I had never seen before. Light shining from behind the strangers silhouetted their forms. They looked like giants. My mind raced. *Who died? What happened? Who are these people? Why are they here? Did I hurt someone? Is my brother hurt?* Choking on my questions, I tried to speak but the only thing I could muster to say was, "Who are you?"

My dad spoke first. He looked directly at me and said, "Son, these two people are here to help you. Your mother and I struggled to do this, but we had no choice." I heard my mom sniffle and whisper, "I'm sorry," as they both exited the bedroom, closing the door behind them.

The room pulsed with silence. The motionless figures were still standing in the same position. The man on the right was a giant and the woman to the left was shorter but equally large in width. They wore matching blue polo shirts, but without my contacts in, I could not make out anything else.

The man boomed with a strong and powerful voice, "Chad, we are not here to hurt you, we are here to help."

The first thought in my head was- *liar! No way you're here to help me.*

This time the lady spoke, "Your parents have decided that your drinking and drug use have gotten out of hand, and they had no choice but to send you to receive help. You're not going to be gone long, just a couple of weeks. If you'll just come with us, everything will be OK."

No! My body went numb. *REHAB! I can't. I can't go to rehab. What about my senior high-school trip, my track season? Everything, everything will be gone.* My thoughts bounced around my head, pulling me in all directions. Still, I did not say a word.

All I could think about was my best friend Bill, who had been shipped off to some institution this same way. He had been woken up in the middle of the night, confronted by an escort team, and whisked away. They locked him up for over a year and threw away the key. He attempted to get away from this same situation but failed. With this in mind, instead of fleeing I complied with their requests and slipped into my clothes.

The three of us stood facing the closed door of my bedroom. On my right side stood the man and to my left was the lady. But I was not so small myself. Standing 6'5" and weighing about two hundred pounds, I knew that I could cause trouble if I decided not to comply. As if reading my mind, the man immediately linked his right arm through my left, and the woman linked her left arm through my right. Their arms were warm and moist, and I could feel their intensity pressed against my skin.

Reaching for the brass knob, the man twisted it to the left and the door popped open. With only the small nightlight guiding our way, we proceeded down the dark hallway. At the end of the hallway, we slowly turned as a single unit at the top of the stairs. The man instructed, "Right foot first," and down we went one step at a time. The steps creaked and cracked with our combined weight in synchronized cadence. At the bottom, the front doors waited eight feet in front of us. These were no ordinary doors. They were intricate wooden doors mixed with detailed glass and carved woodwork. Each door must have weighed at least half a ton and stood twelve feet high. They were powerful and screamed luxury.

I could feel the grips of my escorts tighten. In a matter of seconds we would be outside. Despite their holds, I knew this was my only chance. The man pushed down on the ornate handle and one massive door glided open. With one door cautiously open, he glared at me and said, "Don't walk yet." Rudely keeping his arm locked firmly, he pushed open the other door, sending it swinging in the opposite direction. Shifting his glare back to me, he calmly asked, "OK, Chad, we are going to make this nice and easy, right?" I nodded in agreement, and out the front door we went. As we proceeded down the sidewalk, my adrenaline skyrocketed. This was it! My only chance! I jerked my right shoulder forward, my left back, twisting from the hips to the left. The arm locks broke and I was free. Numb with adrenaline, I leapt into a sprint. Freedom was in my reach. *Just a few more steps and I'm gone.*

SLAM! My body buckled and my neck twisted as my face met the dirt. It happened so quickly, I never saw it coming. It was the equivalent of an unsuspecting quarterback being sacked by a professional lineman. *What happened? No, no, no, I was free...*

Sprawled on the ground, dirt pressed deep in to my cheek, pieces of mulch swam through my mouth and clumps of dust blurred my vision. The weight of the man pressed on top of my back with his unforgiving grip wrapped around my waist. Refusing to give up, I pulled my right arm back under my body into a push-up position. My left arm already folded underneath, I struggled to flip it into a pressing position. With adrenaline fueling my muscles, I pushed with both palms. Either the world was going to move or I was going to get up. Nothing could stand in my way. Freedom or death. Rehab was not an option.

Pulling and dragging my sprawled right leg through the dirt and up toward my chest the man demanded, "STOP RESISTING! STOP RESISTING!" Spit spattered my face. His breath was hot; I could feel the fury in his voice.

I thrust my other leg forward, stomping my foot flat to the ground. He was losing his hold. If I continued to twist, I could break his grip. I dropped my knees, and then exploded up, twisting to the left. He lost his balance and fell backward, taking me with him. With a thud, we hit the ground. His grip broke and I quickly rolled off, scrambling to get to my feet. But before I regained my balance he sprang like a tiger, crushing me to my side. The woman joined in and they both lay on top of me. Their combined weight was unbearable. This time there was no moving the massive load. It was over.

"I'm done, I'm done," I shouted.

"Stay still," the man growled back. The woman moved to the side, and the man leaned back enough to force his forearm onto the back of my neck, squashing my face once again into the mulch. With a strong grip on my right hand, the woman twisted my arm behind my back. The man stood up, twisted my left arm behind my back and slapped a pair of cuffs around my wrists. The man next slipped his left arm between my chest and the ground. With his right arm, he grabbed the chain between the cuffs and in one motion jerked my 200 pound frame easily to my feet. Pain shot up and down my wrists. *Something is extremely wrong with these cuffs,* I thought.

"Ouch, ouch! These hurt. What's wrong with these?"

With little remorse, the man replied, "The cuffs might be twisted. Now walk forward to the car." He gave me a light shove while the woman ran ahead. She opened the door to the gold Ford Taurus and waited. It wasn't until my bare feet met the rough cement of the sidewalk that I realized my shoes were gone, but this was the last problem on my mind. Placing his hand on my head, the man shoved me sideways into the backseat until I was completely stuffed inside. The door slammed shut.

Why, why, why me? What the hell is going on? I don't deserve this. I'm just a kid. What did I do? What's happening? What? Why?

The stinging pain from the cuffs became unbearable. No more questions of why or what. The pain flooded all thoughts and I had to say something. Screaming, I demanded "Take these off, NOW." Silence. They didn't say a word. Not even a glance back. Instead the car shifted into drive and we zoomed off. The streets were quiet, calm, and clear. Not a soul on the road, not the usual Monday morning. The sun had not risen yet, but the eerie orange glow from the neighborhood lamps helped guide the way.

I twisted, fidgeted, lay down, sat up, and moved from one side to the other, but nothing gave any relief from the punishing cuffs digging into my wrists. After several minutes, I finally gave up. My hands had gone numb and with an acknowledgement of defeat, I thumped my head against the passenger door and peered through the window. I accepted the pain and blocked out the burn.

About ten minutes later my trance was broken. The car slowed down, turning into a Waffle House parking lot. Familiar smells of grease and ketchup flooded my nostrils. I couldn't help but think of all the late nights my buddies and I spent eating huge amounts of food to help soak up the booze saturating our blood streams.

As soon as the woman parked the car the man hopped out. He opened the back door and said, "OK, Chad, I know those cuffs are hurting. I'm willing to adjust them, but only if you promise not to do anything funny."

"Yes, yes, of course. I'm done fighting. Just fix these things, please."

He instructed, "OK, lie down on your stomach so I can get to them." I immediately flopped down with my face buried in the cloth seat. The woman opened the other door and held me down. *Clink, clank, snap!* The cuffs came loose and the pain diminished. *Click, clink, clack!* The cuffs were back on, but they were not as tight and didn't hurt. As the doors closed on either side, the only thing that mattered was the welcome relief from the cuffs. The car started again and the journey resumed.

The streets were quiet, hardly a soul on the road. The sun still had not shown its face. I had never seen these streets so bare and calm. Normally, Atlanta streets would have bumper to bumper traffic with people honking and changing lanes for no good reason. But at five in the morning, the streets told a different story. It was odd, but I didn't really care. I rested my head back against the cloth headrest and closed my eyes, hoping to awaken to find myself sprawled out in my bed and this all being a horrible dream.

I slowly dozed off, but was awakened shortly by the man's voice. He was talking to me. My eyes slowly adjusted. Peering though thin gold-framed glasses, the man stared right at me. I was able to get a good look at him now. He was a black man with a bald head, smooth skin, a round face, kind eyes but a serious expression.

"Chad," he calmly said, "my name is Ian and this is Norma. We work for a company that helps teenagers. What we are hired to do is to escort teens, like yourself, to a better place where you can receive the help you need. We are only here to help you. Unfortunately, you have been on the wrong path for some time and need some assistance to place you back where you should be. This is where we come in. We are not part of the institution to where you are going. Our only duties are to ensure you reach your destination safely. Your parents love you very much and would not have done this if they did not care about you and your wellbeing. I know it's hard for you to see this, but you must trust me. Now, do you have any questions?"

I sat there for a moment, digesting everything he said. I didn't have any fight left. My emotions had gone from anger and fear to calm and forlorn acceptance. I did have one question. I quietly muttered, "Do you know how long I'm going to be gone?"

He replied, "I believe it is only for a few weeks."

A sense of relief washed over me. *I can handle this. It's just a few weeks and then I'll be back to my normal life.* I lay my head back against the seat once again and closed my eyes.

This same morning I was supposed to be waking up and going on my high school senior trip. Our school had a magazine sale every year and if we reached a certain dollar amount, the class was rewarded with a trip. I attended a private Christian school that relied big time on this sale to have funds to improve our campus. I never imagined I would be in handcuffs driving somewhere with an escort service the morning of my trip.

After about an hour's drive, I was abruptly awakened by the car's vibrations combined with a loud rumbling noise. I peeled my head back off the glass window and waited for my eyes to create a clear picture. The morning dew on the windows sparkled with the slight hint of the sun's rays reflecting off the tiny drops. "Where are we?" I muttered.

"Hartsfield Airport," Ian replied. That loud rumbling noise must have been a jet airliner taking off over our heads. *Great,* I thought to myself, *the airport. I'm in for it now.*

We drove around the airport for a few minutes, veering off in various directions before we pulled up to a gate. Norma rolled down the window and pressed the green round button, producing a small ticket. The gate rose and we drove in. She drove around the deck passing several spots until she found an area that was a little more secluded from the rest. The car came to a stop, and Ian and Norma sat there for a moment discussing a few things. After a couple minutes, they both stepped out of the vehicle and opened my door. Ian helped me wiggle out of the car. The three of us stood in the orange glow cast down from the parking deck lights. Ian peered at me seriously through his gold-framed glasses and declared, "We are now in the federal jurisdiction. If you decide to run, I will not be able to do anything to help. The airport officers will arrest you and charge you with federal crimes." He paused for a moment before continuing, "I am going to take the cuffs off and we are going to walk through the airport in a civil manner. Now, will you comply and do as I have told you?"

Solemnly, I muttered, "I'm not going anywhere."

"Good." He reached into his pocket, pulled out a little metal clip, and popped open the cuffs. Wow, what a relief. I immediately pulled my hands up in front of my face and looked at the thick red impressions on each wrist. I slowly rubbed them, attempting to bring life back into my hands as Ian looked down and said, "Sorry about the wrists, man."

Looking back with a sharp expression, I replied, "They're fine."

Norma walked over behind the car and popped open the trunk. She pulled out a black book bag and placed it on the cement ground. The bag was my school book bag. *How? What? No way.*

"Your parents packed some things for you." She brought it over, unzipped it and showed me the contents. "Let's see, we've got a pair of shoes," she pulled them out and plopped them on the ground. *Shoot!* I was hoping my bare feet would prevent us from flying. Next, she pulled out a few more things: my MP3 player, headphones, a book, contacts, and a change of clothes. Suddenly, random memoires made sense. The night before when I was going to bed, I noticed my book bag lying by the washing machine. Since I had not placed it there, I thought it strange that the bag had found its way there. I even picked it up for some reason, thinking it was light. But I didn't care enough to investigate. I was too occupied with monitoring my parents to see if they were getting ready for bed.

My parents slept on the main floor and my room was on the second floor. Peering through the living room windows, I watched for the light in their bedroom to disappear. Once that light went off, I immediately went to my room. This time was my favorite part of the day. I pulled out my stash of weed from under the fuzzy coconut man, sat down at my desk, and split open a cheap cigar. Next, I dumped out the tobacco, ground up the weed, and rerolled the cigar into a little piece of heaven. I had a window in my bedroom that opened onto a flat piece of the roof where I would smoke in peace. Even if it were raining, there was a little overhang that sheltered me. I sometimes spent hours up on the roof, thinking about all sorts of different things. Since it was always in the middle of the night, the night noises were always interesting, especially when I was stoned. Once in a while, in the faint distance, I would hear what sounded like a group of rallying people. Our house sat up on a hill so I could hear noises from long distances. To this day I swear that it was a KKK rally. We lived in Forsyth County and rumor has it the KKK started here and that Klan meetings are still not uncommon.

My thoughts were broken by Norma's voice. "Here," she held out my contact case, "your parents said you would want these."

"Yea," I muttered as I grabbed the case. I twisted open the case and popped in the contacts. My vision is not terrible, but still, I can't make out much in the distance without aid from the lenses. After blinking a few times, I could clearly see all around. Norma set the book bag down, zipped it closed, and then lifted it with the straps facing me. I slipped my arms through the straps. As we walked, Ian was on my left and Norma on my right. By this point I had no intention of running and was just going with the flow.

After a ten minute walk through the parking garage, up and down escalators and across the five lanes of traffic filled with taxis, limos, and loved ones bidding farewell, we passed through sliding glass doors and into the busy airport. People raced by on either, carrying their briefcases or rolling their suitcases across the marble floor. Everyone looked worried as they studied the monitors of departures and arrivals or glanced over their tickets, constantly checking their watches.

We didn't have any luggage so we proceeded down the open hallway until we reached the security checkpoint. The line to get to metal detectors snaked around and around for at least thirty yards. But before we got in line, Norma instructed we step off to the side for a moment. She unzipped her fanny pack and produced two boarding passes and forty dollars and handed them to Ian. She declared, "Well, this is where my path ends." She paused for a moment, looking straight into my eyes. "I wish the best of luck to you, Chad. You seem like a real genuine guy, and I know you will come out a better man after this is all over."

I won't lie; she seemed sincere. I looked back in her eyes, but had nothing to say other than, "OK." She turned to Ian, nodded her head and off she went, walking down the long open hallway.

"All right, man, let's get in line." We slowly inched our way through the line until we were faced by the Guardian of the Airport, a short fat black woman. Bold and stern, she demanded, "Remove your shoes, empty your pockets, and place all items including carry-on luggage in the bins."

Ian and I did as instructed, but before I could approach the metal detector, another woman waved in my direction. "Sir, I'm gonna need you to come to this line." *Of course I'm going to get the special security treatment today. My day couldn't get any better, so why not top it off with an anal probing at the airport?* The woman pointed to the ground and instructed, "Stand over here and place your feet in the painted area." From the metal console, she reached for the magic metal-detecting wand and instructed, "Raise your arms." She grazed the wand up, down, and around my body. The wand made slight screeching noises, but exploded into a *beep, beep, beep* as it passed over my belt. "Take your belt off." I slid the belt off and handed it to her. The woman studied it for a few brief moments, turning it over and over until she was satisfied. "OK, you're all clear." She smiled and handed over the belt. "You can get the rest off your stuff over there with that gentleman," she pointed off in a different direction.

Ian was waiting for me when I reached the designated area and with a concerned tone asked, "You good?"

I muttered, "Fine." After stepping into my shoes, I slipped my arms through the book bag straps, slung it over my shoulders and said, "All right." The lack of sleep was starting to catch up with me. My patience was gone, my head hurt, and my stomach was crying for a morsel of food. Not to mention I was sporting a killer hangover from the fifth of Crown I had killed the night before.

"I'm hungry." I looked over pitifully at Ian as we floated down the escalator.

"I know," he replied. "Once we get to the terminals, we'll find something to eat."

When the escalator ended, we took a hard right until we reached a set of glass doors that enclosed the train. The train transported people from one terminal to another within the airport. As a kid, this was always my favorite part. A few minutes later, a loud rushing sound filled the room as the train appeared. Shrill screeches echoed through the terminal as the train came to a sudden stop right in front of us. The doors slid open and people dumped out like an angry ant hill. We waited for everyone to exit before we stepped into the train.

"CAUTION, CAUTION. THE DOORS ARE CLOSING AND DO NOT REOPEN. PLEASE STEP AWAY FROM THE DOORS," the robotic voice warned. Of course, no one paid attention to the warning and several people hurried on, barely making it through the doors before they slammed shut. I sat there wondering, *What if someone really did get caught in those doors and they really didn't reopen. Would the train just go zooming off, dragging some poor soul, smacking every concrete post until it came to a stop a few minutes later?* A realistic concern, I believe.

"THE TAIN IS APPROACHING CONCOURSE A," the voice interrupted my thoughts. The train came to a sharp stop, almost knocking over those several people who were not holding on for balance, before the doors blew open. Ian tapped my shoulder, nodding his head in the direction of the doors, and said, "Let's go."

I quickly turned, but my vision went dark as a sharp pain splintered down my forehead. The hangover from the night before was too strong. My balance was shaky and my legs went numb, but an arm wrapped around my shoulders. Bit by bit, my vision came back with little circles forming a clearer picture. I looked over to see who had caught me. Ian, of course.

"CAUTION, CAUTION, THE DOORS ARE CLOSING AND DO NOT REOPEN." The voice sent a chill down my spine. "Come on," Ian demanded. He pulled me by the arm and we shot through the doors right before they slammed.

Next thing I knew, Ian had both his hands placed on either side of my shoulders with his arms straight, looking me up and down. Finally he said, "Well, I think you're still alive."

I responded, "I'm fine," but I really wanted to say, "Let go of me."

"Well, let's get you something to eat. You good to walk?"

I nodded in reply.

Up the escalator we went and down the giant hallway, until the sweet smell of bacon and eggs filled my nostrils. What a glorious smell! If there is one thing I love most in this world, it's food. I love to eat. I normally eat about every two hours when I'm awake and if I miss a meal, I am not a happy person. We walked over to the buffet and joined the long line with other travelers. *Oh well, at least we're close.* Ten minutes passed before we were finally faced by the lady behind the glass counter. "Scrambled or fried?" She pointed at two different bins containing the eggs.

"Fried, please," I responded. She slapped two eggs onto a Styrofoam tray and passed it to the next lady.

"Links or patties?"

"Both," I almost drooled, and she dropped the sausages on the tray and passed it.

"Biscuits and gravy, sir?" This time a man asked.

"Yeah," I responded. After adding the biscuits and gravy, he sent the tray to its final destination where another man stood behind a cash register.

"What to drink, sir?"

"Orange juice." Reaching down into a bucket of ice, he pulled out a small plastic bottle orange juice. He practically dropped the bottle on the counter, ricocheting a piece of ice that almost hit me in the face.

"Eight fifty," he announced.

I pointed at Ian. "I'm with him."

"OK, seventeen dollars, then," he moved his glare to Ian. Ian paid the man, and we walked over to the utensil area.

I didn't say a single word or look up as I shoveled the heap of breakfast into my mouth. Ian did the same. He obviously shared my passion for food.

When my plate was clear, I looked up at Ian.

He was leaning back in his chair and smiled a little before saying, "Hit the spot." I reached across the table and grabbed his tray, stacking it on top of mine, and started to get up. His voice went stern, "Hold on, big guy. Hang tight for a minute." His comment reminded me that his job was to make sure I didn't disappear. Oops. It was another escape attempt gone sour.

"My bad." I sat back down. He pulled his book bag to his lap, unzipped it and pulled out some documents. He glanced over the papers, shifting from page to page, and made a few notes. Once finished, he placed the papers back into their manila folder, stuffed it all back in the book bag and checked his watch. "All right man, let's go." I grabbed the trays and off we went to the terminal.

"MAY I HAVE YOUR ATTENTION, PLEASE. FLIGHT 273, NONSTOP TO HELENA, MONTANA, WILL BEGIN BOARDING, STARTING WITH FIRST CLASS. PLEASE HAVE YOUR BOARDING PASSES READY," the lady behind the check-in desk announced over the intercom. Like a deer in headlights, I froze. *Montana! Where on earth am I going?* I panicked and my heart sank as an intense feeling of depression engulfed me. Everything around me seemed to go into slow motion as I scoped out the room. *Maybe I should just run. No, I can't. Do it! Run now! I can do it, I can get away. It would be easy. Wait, no, no. I'm in federal jurisdiction. I would go to jail. Just faint or something. What? No. What do I do? What do I do?* My adrenalin raced, my heart pounded, and fear rushed through my veins. Slowly, cautiously, I started to step back. *This is my last chance. Go!*

"Chad, what's wrong?"

"Aaaah, aaah, nothing," I snapped back to reality and nervously replied, "Just lost in my head."

"We're about to board." And just like turning the heat off to a boiling pot of water, my nerve level dropped back to a stable, accepting, state.

Wow, that was intense. If only Ian had just seen what I was contemplating. Perhaps he had? Instantly an overwhelming sense of anxiety rolled over me. Nervously, I looked over at Ian to see if he was going to pull out his handcuffs. *Maybe he does know. No, not the cuffs, please no.* Much to my relief, he was frantically rummaging through his book bag. *Sweet, maybe he lost the tickets or the IDs.* Hope flooded my thoughts. But nope, my dreams were crushed. He stood up, pulling out the boarding cards and the IDs. Dirt! He handed them to me.

"MAY I HAVE YOUR ATTENTION, PLEASE. FLIGHT 273, NONSTOP TO HELENA, MONTANA, WILL NOW BEGIN BOARDING ROWS 30 THROUGH 33. PLEASE HAVE YOUR BOARDING PASSES AND IDENTIFICATION READY."

I glanced down at my card, Row 3, Seat C. Ian nudged me, "That's us, man," and we joined the line to board the plane.

A female attendant politely asked, "Hello, sir. May I have your boarding pass, please?"

"Here," I handed the cards to her. She paused as she glanced at my face, looked down at the cards, placed them on a scanner and handed them back. "Enjoy your flight, sir." I nodded and slipped into the retractable walkway with Ian right on my tail.

"Good morning, sir," we were greeted by a bubbly flight attendant. She stood smiling with white teeth, long blond hair and blue eyes.

We proceeded down the narrow aisle of the plane, both of us ducking the whole time, until we reached Row 30 near the back of the plane. I slipped my book bag onto the cloth seat, unzipped it, and searched until I felt the rubber cords to my headphones. I pulled out the headphones and MP3 player, zipped the bag closed, and swung it up into the overhead compartment. After looking at the diagram to confirm my spot, I plopped down into Seat F, next to the window.

What a load off. My body was exhausted. The mix of being awakened in the middle of the night, the failed flee attempt, and the overall exhaustion from emotional stress had taken its toll.

I rested my head against the seat and closed my eyes. Something didn't feel right, though. I was missing something. Oh, right, a pillow. But I was not about to move. Opening my eyes, I noticed Ian still standing and fidgeting with his book bag, so I calmly asked, "Hey Ian, will you get us a couple pillows and some blankets?"

"Sure thing," he replied. I leaned my head back into the seat and closed my eyes. I immediately started to slip away into a doze, but was startled by a couple of small pillows dropping into my lap.

"Thanks," I muttered as he sat down and handed me a small blue blanket. I stretched out the blanket, and started twisting and fidgeting and knocking my knees into the seat in front me. No matter how I positioned my body, my legs were lodged against the seat. "Damn, these seats suck," I blurted in frustration.

"Just relax," Ian stated. But I knew he was going to have the same problem. As soon as he sat down, he started fidgeting the same way and conceded, "Man, you're right."

"Told ya." For the moment, I had given up on trying to get comfortable.

I sat staring for a few minutes as Ian got situated. I was curious about him and finally asked, "So, have you always worked for an escort service?"

"Nope," he responded. "I've only been doing this for a few years. I actually used to be a cop."

"Hmm, I see. That sounds about right. So, why the change?"

"Well, I was tired of sending people to jail. I wanted to do something that had a little more purpose to it," he said, looking straight into my eyes.

Before I had a chance to respond, he continued, "I had a friend on the force whose brother overdosed on heroin." He paused for a moment. "My friend was crushed. He completely broke down and ended up quitting the force. He sort of just disappeared and I didn't hear from him for about a year. But one day I got a random phone call and he explained how he had found this new job that involved helping troubled teens. It sounded interesting. The more he explained, the more interested I became, so I ended up applying. About six months later, I received a phone call offering a job. I took the offer and here I am today."

"Hmm, that's pretty cool. So do you enjoy it?"

He focused intently through his glasses right into my eyes. "You know, Chad, I really do." And just like that, the wall between us came crashing down. *This guy really does care about me.* Feelings of anger, aggression, and dislike suddenly morphed into a new sense of fondness. Not wanting to reveal myself though, I replied nonchalantly, "That's interesting."

The airplane was filling and people were settling down, storing their carry-on bags, grabbing pillows, and buckling their seatbelts. Fully encased in a blanket, Ian laid his head against the seat and closed his eyes. I stuck my headphones in, switched on Dave Matthews, shoved my pillow into the corner of the seat and shut my eyes.

The Dub

I practically jumped out of my seat as I was jerked from a deep sleep. My eyes shot open as my weight thrust forward. Everything rumbled, shook, and vibrated. Loud rumbling noises came from the overhead compartments. Luggage bounced and juggled. Seatback trays shook from side to side, the ground vibrated, and a few items ahead in the aisle dropped from an opened bin. The items fell for what seemed like an eternity, until they went bouncing off the floor. *We're crashing, we're crashing! This is it, this is the end!* I panicked.

Frantically, I looked around, expecting everyone else to be panicking and pulling the elastic cords to the oxygen masks. But everyone seemed unusually calm. People were still reading books, looking out the window, pulling out cell phones, and some were even still asleep. Then it hit me, we're landing. *Oh man...What a relief.* I could feel the fear drain from my nerves. I looked over at Ian. He was awake and looking curiously back at me. I must have still had an expression of complete horror on my face because he quickly asked, "You all right, son?"

"Wow, yeah, that scared me. Thought we were crashing for a second.

He chuckled before saying, "Well, you're safe now, man."

The plane was creeping along at a snail's pace as we worked our way down the different taxiways. Just about all the window shades had been raised, except for the random deep sleepers. The morning sun beamed through the windows, lighting up the entire plane. I took a good look out and saw absolute beauty. Snow-covered mountains filled the entire horizon while the glistening sun lit a never-ending forest of green pines. If I looked hard enough toward the top of the mountains, I could see little specks of color, which were homes scattered throughout the mountain range. Toward the bottom were large clusters of homes combined with long roads snaking their way back and forth along the face. Among the clusters an occasional wisp of smoke rose from the chimneys.

What a peaceful sight, I thought to myself. I looked over at Ian. He must have been thinking the same thing, because he had a look of pure serenity smeared all over his face.

Realizing my headphones were still in, I looked down at the music player. I must have listened to three full albums of Dave Matthews before it reached its end and shut off.

The plane jerked to a stop as we reached the gate. The "fasten seat belt" light switched off, the intercom dinged, and everyone jumped out of their seats. They collectively reached up into the overhead compartments, gathered their belongings, took a quick stretch, and looked back in their seat for the possibility of left items. I took my time. Slowly standing up into the aisle, I had to duck as I extended one cramped leg at a time. It felt glorious. Each kneecap cracked and the feeling of freedom was indescribable. Ian and I waited for a few minutes as the line of people inched their way toward the front of the plane.

As we reached the exit door of the plane, the flight attendants and pilots were bidding farewell to the passengers. The same bubbly flight attendant smiled a big fake smile and said, "Have a great day." *Yeah...Fabulous, let me tell you.*

We worked our way through the airport, dodging and swerving around people until we reached the moving sidewalk. After a brisk walk, we came to an intersection with signs pointing in various directions. Ian looked up for a moment before turning left toward baggage claim, still making sure I was by his side at all times. We rounded a final corner and came face to face with groups of people holding up signs. One man was a limo driver holding a sign that read "Smith." To his left was a middle-aged woman with an anxious look. In one hand she held a string attached to a balloon and the other hand held the hand of a little girl. The girl was holding a sign that read "Welcome Home Daddy." I glanced over to the right of the woman and saw an average-sized man with short red hair and a full goatee. He was a thicker man, but what caught my eye was the plain white poster board he held. Scraggily writing had spelled

"Wilderness Treatment Center." Ian was walking right toward him. Everything just got real. *This is it! Oh no!* As we approached the man, my throat tightened. "You must be Ian?" He stuck out his hand.

Ian grasped his hand and responded, "Yes, sir. Carsten, right?"

"You got it," he said with a smile. He looked over at me, stuck out his hand, and said, "And you, sir, must be Chad."

Nervously grabbing his hand, I gave it a weak shake and nodded while muttering, "Yeah."

He turned his attention back to Ian and said, "Well, I presume you have some paperwork for me."

"Yes, sir." Ian quickly slipped off the book bag, unzipped it and pulled out the manila folder along with a pen. "Here we are," he said, adjusting the thin gold frames as he shuffled through the papers. Pulling out a sheet, he handed it to Carsten along with a pen and pointed near the bottom. "Sign at the X please." Carsten paused for a few moments, reading over the document, before nodding in approval. He looked around for a surface to write on before he finally stuck the paper on his thigh, scribbled on the sheet, and handed it back. Ian slipped the paper into the folder and stuffed it back in his bag. There was an awkward moment of silence. Ian broke it by sticking out his hand toward me and said, "Best of luck to you." I grasped his hand and looked away into the distance. With a firm grasp, he held on tightly, not letting go. Both of his rough, thick hands swallowed my hand. Ian's powerful voice pulled my gaze into his eyes. "I encourage you to make the best of this situation. You are a strong young man, and from what I can tell, you have a big heart. Your parents think the world of you, so don't let them, or yourself, down."

Nodding, I replied, "All right, man," and he released my hand. Ian turned and walked off, leaving me with Carsten.

Carsten gave a crooked smile and said, "All right, let's go. Follow me." Off we went through the sliding glass doors and out into the fresh mountain air. The air was cold, crisp, thin and very refreshing. Accumulations of snow were scattered along the concrete railings, bushes, trash cans, and random cold spots. The sun was out and starting to warm the frigid ground. Stepping off the curb into the street, I squished into black slush. Passing cars had churned the salt, dirt, and who-knows-what-else, creating a nasty black mixture along the side of the road. It made a city look like a dump. And that is exactly how the Ford Explorer looked we were approaching. Like a dump. Once upon a time, this vehicle surely had a nice shiny coat. Now it was tired, clearly worn from the black slush combined with years of transporting individuals from the airport. Carsten pointed and said, "Hop in." He crossed to the driver's side while I pulled on the rusted silver handle. The creaking vibration of the door opening sent a slab of slush falling to the ground, splattering over my shoes. I shook it off disgustedly and jumped in. Carsten turned the key in the ignition, slipped the explorer in drive and we zoomed off.

We rode in mutual silence for awhile. I eventually broke the standoff by nervously asking, "So, this is like a two week program, right."

He looked a bit confused and replied, "No, this program lasts two months."

"What? No! I was told I would only be gone for two weeks." He didn't respond so I started again, "I mean, it's possible to finish in two weeks, just most finish in two months, right?" I was becoming extremely worried.

After an eternity he finally responded, "Nope. Everyone is here for two months."

"Shit!"

Carsten looked over for a second but focused back on the road. An eerie feeling pulsed through my body as I became frantic. *Two months, two months, that's forever! I'll never make it! No way. This blows!* Trying to sift through his words, I slumped my head against the side window. *That can't be right. Surely he's lying. Right?*

The road was long and straight, flanked by towering mountain ranges on either side. We were the only ones traveling on the bare road except for the occasional semi truck pulling a trailer full of massive, fresh-cut trees. We zoomed around them, leaving their slow progress as only specks in the rearview mirror. Every couple minutes the wipers went flying across the windshield as a green fluid sprayed everywhere. A stream of the fluid flowed in the wind from the top of the windshield all the way to the side, and back down until it was blown off. I was irritated by all the spraying so I calmly asked, "What's up with the constant windshield cleaning?"

He explained, "The combination of salt, slush, and other chemicals on the road creates a film. If I don't, I won't be able to see a thing."

"Ah, I see." After that I didn't really have much else to say. Apparently he didn't either, so we continued down the never-ending road in silence.

Two hours later, my wandering thoughts were broken by the clicking noise of the left turn signal blinking on and off. The car was slowing, so I perked up to see what was going on. He made a left turn onto an unpaved road. We passed an old wooden sign with faded letters that read "Wilderness Treatment Center." The car jumped and bumped as we slowly drove along the poor road. A unique fence stood along the sides of the road. The fence was constructed of small posts and shaved tree rails about four feet long. It didn't seem to serve any purpose except decoration. Behind the fences were large, flat snow-covered fields absent of any visible animal life.

After five minutes of tussling and bumping, we turned right and drove under a wooden arch that also read "Wilderness Treatment Center." In the distance I could see several structures that became clearer as we approached. On the right hand side I saw five log cabins all in a line, a separate worn building, and a small house. All the buildings were covered in snow. Directly in front of us was an old red barn along with several fenced- in areas containing horses and cows. To the left was another small building and a tiny little cabin. The car pulled up to the small one-story building on the left, Carsten put the vehicle in park and said, "OK, let's go." Reluctantly, I ambled out and followed him. He opened the building's glass door and instructed, "Walk to the back." The worn carpet in the narrow dim hallway was tired and smelled musty. On my left and on my right we passed door frames that opened up to small rooms with faded wood paneling on the walls and old blue chairs positioned in a circle. The rooms were identical with two windows, beaming light into the circle of chairs. As we reached the end of the building, I looked back at Carsten. The light shining from the front glass door only allowed me to see the outline of his body.

His order was eerie as he instructed, "Go into the bathroom and into the stall." *What on earth are we doing? This is weird. This can't be right. Whatever, just do it.* I pushed open the old wooden door and stepped into the stall. Reaching to the top of the cream-colored door, he pulled it shut, separating us. He calmly ordered, "OK, take off your shirt, pants, shoes and socks, and slide them under the door." *What the...? Why am I undressing! This is wrong.* I thought about refusing, but then again I was at a rehab facility. Nothing was right... I did as instructed and stood on the cold tile with nothing on but my boxer shorts. As I waited, I looked down at the rusty drain hole where the faded green tile sloped together. My belt clicked and clanked as he shook my jeans, sifted through the pockets, and shook the shirt. "OK, come on out here." Still feeling awkward, I stepped out. "Now take your thumbs and run them along your underwear straps all the way around your body." He watched. Satisfied, he said, "OK, you can get dressed now." *Thank God!* Every second that passed made me more nervous. I slipped back into my clothes and tied my shoes.

"All right, follow me." Right on his heels, I followed him into a tiny room with a wooden desk and yet another blue plastic chair across from it. The same wood paneling encased the walls and in the upper portion of the wall, directly in front, a small window allowed enough light to feed a long stringy plant that crept all the way down the wall.

Waving his hand toward the blue plastic chair, he instructed, "Take a seat." He plopped into a tired leather swivel chair, switched on the desk lamp and pulled out a file with my name written across the top. Before he opened it, he reached for the black desk phone. Looking at me, he said, "I need to call your parents to let them know you arrived safely." I merely nodded my head. "After I have spoken with them, I will give you the opportunity, if you'd like, that is, to talk to them." I didn't respond. He started dialing. *Ring, ring, ring.* I could hear the phone buzzing, or was that my heart? Who knows, but one thing was for sure. I was instantly furious. *Screw them. How could they do this!*

"Good evening, this is Steve," my dad answered and before Carsten could respond, I heard my mom pick up and frantically say, "Hello, hello?"

"Hello, Mr. Hepler and Mrs. Hepler. This is Carsten with Wilderness Recovery Institution."

My dad spoke nervously, "Yes, yes. How are you, sir?"

"Just fine." Carsten was calm. "I am calling to let you know I have Chad sitting here with me. Everything went as planned and he arrived safely a few moments ago."

"Excellent," my dad sounded better. My mom sighed in relief, "Oh, wow, that's great."

With the phone still pressed to his cheek, Carsten looked at me, "I'm going to give Chad the opportunity to talk to you now." He held out the phone. *Hell no. There is no way I'm talking to them. Screw this and screw them.* I shook my head, anger displayed on my face. He spoke back into the phone, "OK, Mr. and Mrs. Hepler, he does not feel like speaking at the moment, but we will be in touch."

At almost a whisper level, my mom spoke, "OK, Carsten, thank you."

"Take care." Carsten placed the phone back on the receiver. "Let's go." He stood up and I followed. We passed back through the glass door, across a frozen sidewalk and up a couple warped wooden stairs into a small grey trailer. Carsten held the door open as I stepped in. We immediately faced two women sitting behind giant wooden desks. The same wooden paneling encased the room, but it was in worse shape. Random strips had fallen off and a few holes were scattered throughout. Carsten pointed to yet another blue plastic chair next to the door and instructed, "Have a seat." *Blue plastic chairs! Are they following me? Haunting me?* The chairs symbolized support groups and made me squirm. Reluctantly, I sat down and Carsten disappeared. Quietly waiting, I slumped in the chair and wallowed in confusion. *Where am I? This is nuts! Who are these people?*

A few moments later, Carsten reappeared wheeling a giant box on a dolly and plopped it in front of me. "All right, let's see what we got." He cut the box open.

Curious, I asked "What's this?"

From one knee he looked up. "Your stuff."

Huh? How did I have stuff here? Am I dreaming? It took a minute, but I realized my parents must have mailed some of my belongings. The first thing Carsten pulled out was a new pair of boots. He plopped them down on the floor and said, "Here, put these on. You're gonna want them." They were chunky and awkward, but I slipped off my wet tennis shoes and pulled on the boots. They felt good, nice and warm. He kept pulling out stuff: clothing, toiletries, a towel, pad of paper, pens, a Bible, a calling card, a magazine, a portable CD player, and two greeting cards. He threw the magazine and CD player back in a separate container and said, "You will get those back when you leave." *Whatever.* I stayed silent. Then he went through my book bag, pulling out the MP3 player and tossed it in the container as well. "OK, we're gonna leave this stuff here for a minute." He stood up and instructed, "Follow me." With every step creaking, we crossed through the groaning trailer room until we reached a small office with a lady sitting behind a desk. "This is Ms. Denise, our nurse. She's gonna check you out for a minute."

"Have a seat please," she said with a smile. I sat down in a cloth chair. Thank goodness! For a moment I forgot I was at rehab as she went through the standard medical questions and procedures, had me sign a few forms, and took my blood before calling Carsten back into the room. With a bandage over my forearm, I got up and followed Carsten back to the room where my clothes lay next to the box they came in.

He instructed, "All right, put your stuff back in the box and bring it with you." I packed the items and picked up the giant box. We went out the front door, down the wooden stairs, turned left and passed through a ten-foot opening in the fence. He stopped. "Before we go any further, let me point out some boundaries," he stared at me to make sure I was paying attention. "At no time are you allowed back past this point, unless you are with a staff member or instructed to do so by a staff member." I nodded my head and he continued, "The fence you see around the fields," he pointed all around the area, "are the boundaries. Once again, at no time are you allowed outside that area unless you are with a staff member or for some reason instructed by a staff member to be out there." He looked right at me, waiting for an acknowledgment.

"Got it," I quickly replied.

"Good. Let's go." I followed as we worked our way down the slippery sidewalk, passing cabins 1, 2, 3, until we reached cabin 4. We went up a few stairs, past some wooden rocking chairs and through a noisy screen door. As we entered the cabin the fresh smell of pine overwhelmed my senses. It was a relaxing, woodsy smell that reminded me of a ski lodge.

To my left were four bunk beds made of shaven trees and thick logs. To my right were four more bunk beds with one bunk without sheets. He pointed at the bare bunk and instructed, "Put your box up there." I threw the box on the top bunk and followed Carsten outside. He paused for a minute to look at his watch. "On Fridays we have what's called 'work day.'" *Great! Work day...* "Right now it's three thirty, so there is another hour left." With a slight smile he said, "Follow me." We stepped off the sidewalk into a foot of snow and marched around the cabin until we came to a tiny, old white house. It was no wider than twenty feet with crooked siding boards. Peeling paint strips covered the boards. Carsten pulled open the half-hung wooden door and a surge of warm air mixed with laundry detergent engulfed us. Inside the room were two young males and one female. The female was short and slim with frizzy red and blond hair.

Carsten announced, "Jenna, this is Chad. He is a new addition here to help."

Jenna looked stunned standing there holding a pile of sheets. She turned to the washing machine, stuffed in the sheets, and finally said, "Hello." Her eyes were as blue as the afternoon sky, but looked tired and spacey. I glanced at Carsten, but he was already walking out the door. She gave a little sigh, shifted her gaze over to the two males who were fumbling with a bed sheet and attempting to fold it. She said, "You can join them."

I looked at them. They were joking and laughing, attempting to fold the sheet. I felt awkward and out of place, but stepped over to them and asked, "Aah, so, what should I do?"

One of them pointed at a hamper full of bed sheets, "Well, we have to fold these." I reached in and held up one of the tired white sheets, folded it into a nice neat square, and placed it in a separate hamper with other folded sheets. I didn't really know what to say, so I just kept folding. Still stunned and out of place, I felt depressed, confused, scared. I could not comprehend where I was.

There were only four sheets left to fold. Once I finished, I placed them on the shelves with the rest of the sheets. Unsure of what to do next, I just stood there. Finally, I introduced myself to one of the guys, "I'm Chad, by the way."

He looked at me with an interested look. He was average height, slim, with defined cheekbones. His eyes were as dark as coal, his hair was spiky, and he was wearing worn, holey jeans with a faded black t-shirt, but what really stood out were his ear lobes. They looked just like a cat's butt. His ears must have been pierced and then stretched out to hold a bigger ring. I had seen band members do this before and always wondered what would happen when they realized they couldn't wear them anymore. Now I knew and it looked ridiculous. With a scratchy voice, he said, "What's up? I'm Steven, but call me Fritz."

With a sinister laugh, he announced, "Welcome to the Dub, the greatest place on earth."

"The Dub?" Confused, I looked at him.

"Yeah, dude, the Dub. That's what we all call it."

"Why's that?"

"Wilderness Treatment Center, the Dub, like W. Get it?" He waited for a response.

"Ah, yes, gotcha. Yeah."

By this point the other guy seemed interested in our conversation. He was standing a little behind Fritz, but stepped around and said, "Hey man, I'm Stan."

"Chad," I reached out to shake his hand before seeing they were bandaged. He held his hands up to show they weren't operable. "Damn, what happened?"

"Frost bite." He unwrapped a couple strips of cloth to show two swollen black and blue fingers full of pus and at least four times the size of a normal finger.

"Wow, that's crazy," I stood there staring in shock. "How'd it happen?"

"The Trip." He stared straight into my eyes.

"The Trip? What's that?"

"It sucks. You'll have to do it. It's a sixteen-day trip where you cross-country ski three to five miles every day and live in the freezing cold. When we went, we got stuck in a four-day blizzard with minus-twenty-degree temperatures."

Fritz joined in, "Yeah, dude, it blows. I wanted to shoot myself. The wind and cold were unbearable."

Stan interrupted, "Yeah, but when you go it'll be in March, so it won't be as cold at least."

I stood digesting everything they had just said. *Sixteen days, sixteen days.* It kept rolling around in my mind. That's a long time to be in the woods. I was getting nervous just thinking about it. Curious, I asked, "So where do you shower?"

They both laughed. Stan replied, "A shower? No shower, and you only change clothes once." Fritz was still laughing and Stan continued, "Just wait—you'll smell so bad, it'll make you nauseous."

Jenna interrupted our conversation, "OK, boys, we're done here. Let's go to the kitchen." She pushed open the wooden door and walked outside toward the back of a separate larger building. As we stomped through the snow, we passed a pile of shaved logs that were each about fifteen feet in length. They were the only things around that didn't have snow covering them. As we were stepping into a giant kitchen, I asked Fritz, "Hey, what's up with the pile of logs?"

He looked back with smile and said, "Those suck. When you get in trouble, you have to peel the bark off of one. You take this dull piece of metal that's shaped like a boomerang with handles on either side and you strip the bark off piece by piece." He demonstrated the movement. "I've peeled like fifty," he added.

I muttered, "Damn, that sucks."

We were all standing around in the kitchen, waiting for instructions while Jenna was bending over to pick up some large cans. With a mischievous smile Fritz quickly looked over at Stan. Stan nodded back. Fritz wound his hand back above his head and came swinging down, smacking Jenna in the rear. She jumped forward and let out a little yelp. "Ouch, you shit head!" She stood up, looking irritated. "That's a log for you."

"Yeah, right." Fritz laughed uncontrollably.

Jenna shrugged it off and pointed at Stan. "You come open these." She dropped a box full of giant aluminum cans onto the stainless steel counter and pulled out an industrial-sized can opener.

Stan looked at her like she was crazy. "Now how do you suppose I open those with no fingers?"

"Oh shit," she instantly realized her mistake. Shifting her attention to me, she nicely asked, "Chad, will you open these?"

"Yeah, no problem."

After thirty minutes of prepping the food, the work day was over. Fritz told me it was time to go back to the cabins for an hour before dinner. We marched back to the cabins as other boys appeared from all directions. They hooted and hollered with smiles smeared all over their faces. Everyone seemed to be in good spirits, except me. I stepped into the cabin to find it full of young guys standing around in dirty work clothes talking amongst themselves. Crossing over to my bunk, I could feel the curious stares following me. Just as I was reaching up to grab my box, I heard the screen door slam shut and an excited voice say, "Chad, sweet! You're in my cabin." Fritz stood shirtless, a cigarette stuck into each of the butt holes in his ear lobes. I nodded and he announced, "Hey, losers, this is Chad, the newest addition to the Dub." I looked around the room at all the faces. Everyone gave me a little acknowledgment in the form of a nod, a slight wave or just eye contact. I felt a little more comfortable, but nervousness still rumbled in my chest. Keeping to myself for the moment, I made my bed.

The irritation and anger about being shipped off was starting to get to me. Confused and angry, I couldn't handle the reality of the situation. I hopped down from my bunk, reared my leg back, and kicked the box. It somersaulted across the room. "Screw this," I blurted and stormed out of the cabin onto the porch. I needed fresh air or something. *Why, why? Where am I? This is terrible.* Plopping into one of the rocking chairs, I lowered my head into my hands. I kept thinking about what I was going to miss: my school trip, prom, graduation, and my senior track season.

This was supposed to be my year. I was the best pole-vaulter at school. I had broken the twenty-three-year-old school record and won regional. I received a colored picture on the front page of the newspaper along with an article about how I helped the team win the regional meet. I placed second at state and was thirsty to come back as state champion.

Was I really going to miss that? Two months? Well, maybe I'll be back. I don't know. The realization of not competing pushed a dagger straight in to my heart. Confused, I kept thinking, *Why, why, why would my parents do this to me?* They knew how important my track season is to me. It doesn't make sense. Why wouldn't they just wait until I graduated? Lost, hurt, and alone, I agonized in confusion. There was nothing I could do about it. Slowly lifting my sulking head, I watched large flakes of snow fall silently to the ground.

"It's beautiful, isn't it?" Another guy plopped into the rocking chair next to me and lit up a cigarette.

I wasn't in the mood for conversation but mustered a reply, "Sure is."

Letting the cigarette rest between his lips, he introduced himself, "I'm Rob."

"Chad." I stared at the falling snow.

"So you're the new guy, huh?"

"Guess so." I was starting to get irritated.

"Well, at least you came on a good night." I looked at him like he had lost his mind, so he clarified, "Tonight is movie night, the only night we get some sort of entertainment."

How lucky, I thought, but I didn't respond. We sat in silence for a couple minutes as he puffed down the cigarette. Out of the corner of my eye, I saw the cigarette fly through the air. He stood up, turned toward the door, and said, "All right, man, when the bell rings, it will be time for dinner."

I didn't respond. I was too wrapped up in my thoughts. My stare betrayed my inner helplessness. I sat for another few minutes. The railings, sidewalk, and rooftops were covered in a fresh three inches of snow. It was peaceful, but I couldn't appreciate it. My mind was depressed.

Eventually the cold took its toll and I went back into the cabin. I spotted my box, looking thoroughly defeated from where I kicked it. I bent over, snatched it up and carried it to my bedside. I pulled out the large blue winter coat sitting on top and set it aside to wear to dinner. I turned the box and dumped out the remaining contents. After methodically sorting through the different clothes and items, I began placing the contents on the shelves. The two greeting cards I had seen earlier caught my attention. It was time to read them. I jumped up onto the bed, bringing the cards with me. The first card was a birthday card from my father. My eighteenth birthday was in three days. How ironic that Dad would give me a Happy Birthday card, considering they just ripped me out of bed and shipped me off. Opening the card, I read only what was written on the back.

My son, Chad

We always make a wish on our birthdays and here are some of my wishes to share with you.

*I wish you were here to celebrate your birthday.
*I wish you didn't drink and drive—it will eventually end in a critical crash.
*I wish I didn't have to make these types of decisions.
*I wish we would hug more.
*I wish I could talk more openly to you—and you to me.
*I wish man never created alcohol.
*I wish good health to you always.
*I wish man never created drugs.
*I wish we would spend more time together.

*But my biggest wish is that this program can help you get a new start.

Chad, I will always be there for you. . . just as I am today.

> *All my love,*
> *Dad*

Setting the card down, I did everything I could to hold back the emotions. My dad and I never had conversations that dealt with feelings. Not like this. These words were saturated with emotions. It was overwhelming. Anger, frustration, and sadness were the only emotions I'd been feeling, but that card...that card only held love. *No, be angry. They just sent you to rehab.* But every heart-piercing statement echoed through my brain. I looked up at the ceiling and tried to hide my emotions. Quickly blinking my eyes, I pushed it all back down.

The other card could only be worse. I picked it up and, pausing for a moment, took in a deep breath and let out a sigh. Opening the card, my eyes fell to my mom's chicken scratch writing on the bottom of the right side.

Dear Chad,

I love you so very much, Chad. I remember the day you were born. As I held you, I could not stop smiling. I knew that in my heart God had given me the best gift ever. I have never forgotten that moment. The only difference is that my love is deeper for you. This has proven to be a very hard world to grow up in...much harder than the world I grew up in. This was very hard for us to do, but you will not understand until you are a parent. We did everything we knew to do to help you, but nothing seemed to be working. We do not want you to have a deadly accident while you are under the influence of alcohol or drugs, or the combination. If you continued that way you did during <u>Christmas break something would have eventually happened</u>. It was only a matter of time. It seemed like you had completely forgotten the danger of driving under the influence. Only you know the amount you are using. Please be truthful with the people that want to help you. Figure out how to live your life without the substances you've been using to have fun. Think about your future. You have so many talents and accomplishments. And most importantly, you have a good heart and care deeply about people. We love you dearly. I will be praying for you as always.

Love, Mom
P.S. We will miss you terribly.

Laying the card on the bed, I gazed around the room in a dead stare, digesting everything she said. Tears bubbled up. The anger, the pain had regained control, but the love...the love smacked me in the heart. The contradicting emotions were tugging and twisting. I could feel my eyes turning red from emotional overload. A tear was coming. *Not now. I can't cry now. Not in front of these guys. What will they think? They'll laugh at me, poke fun. I can't cry. My reputation will be ruined.* I tried to shove everything down. Think about something else, anything—anything but the potent mixture of emotions. Trees, beaches, the wall. I blocked everything out. Shoved it down, buried it, bottled it up, pushed it aside. The swelling was reducing and still not a stray tear. I blinked my eyes and felt nothing. I had done it. My emotions were stabilizing.

After the emotional distress completely passed, I lay my head back onto my pillow. What a battle. Looking up at the ceiling, I thought about all the things my parents had mentioned. All the points relating to my drinking and drug use were unclear. Were they right? I don't know, but I had to see. I shoved in the tape of blurry memories and pressed play.

Memories

It was five days before my seventeenth birthday, my junior year of high school. A buddy and I were hanging out at a local spot, shooting pool and having a good time, when we walked out into the parking lot and my eyes caught sight of two one hundred dollar bills just lying on the black asphalt. I couldn't believe it. Quickly glancing around, I didn't see any one else, so I snatched up the bills. I couldn't believe my luck.

Deciding the best thing to do with the money was to buy a bag of weed, I immediately called up one of my dealers and bought half an ounce. Holding the bag, I debated whether I should just smoke it or sell the majority of it to buy a larger bag. The idea of selling weed to smoke for free sounded fantastic. Visions of being a weed dealer danced through my brain.

Over the next couple days my time was spent driving around suburbia from deal to deal. Two nights into my Pablo Escobar campaign, I got a standard call to meet a customer in a restaurant parking lot right outside the mall. Before going, I weighed out five different bags, placed them in Ziploc sandwich bags, and stuffed them in my coat pocket. Everything was great. I was smoking for free and making money.

Cruising down one of the mall roads, not really paying attention, I passed two cop cars lurking along the side of the road. They were sitting in the dark with all their lights off. When I noticed them, I glanced at my speedometer. I was going fifteen over. One of the cops' headlights lit up and pulled right behind me as I sat at a red light. *No way. I am not getting pulled over.* The light turned green and the blue lights lit up. I panicked. My nerves went numb with fear. *Have to look calm. Have to look calm.* Obeying every tiny law, I slowly and calmly pulled into a restaurant parking lot. The police car parked right behind me. Stoned out of my mind, I panicked and threw open the door. "SIR, DO NOT MOVE. REMAIN IN THE VEHICLE," the loudspeaker echoed through my car. Sitting frozen in fear with all lights shining on me, I tried to appear innocent. Cautiously approaching my car, the officer shined a flashlight into my eyes. The light forced me to squint and I couldn't see a thing, I could only hear her voice. Stern and direct, she asked, "Good evening, sir. May I see your driver's license and proof of insurance, please?" Her voice heightened my anxiety as I fumbled through the armrest compartment, searching frantically for my wallet. *Where is it? Where is it? It's not here! Oh no.* I searched my brain, but I was too stoned to think and the nervousness didn't help. Finally, in a moment of clarity, I realized my wallet was in the inside pocket of the door.

"Aaah, sure, my wallet is in there." I pointed to the pocket of the door that was still open.

"OK, go ahead and get it."

Reaching down, I pulled back the cloth pocket and grabbed the wallet. My impaired brain had forgotten about a bag of weed stuffed in the pocket. I saw it, but prayed she didn't. With shaky hands, I slipped my driver's license and insurance card out of the wallet and handed them to the officer. She held up her flashlight, pointing the light down on the cards, paused for a moment and said, "All right, hang tight." Immediately my mind flooded with more anxiety, but still I remained hopeful and prayed she would just write a ticket and be on her way.

Fifteen minutes crept by. Then a K-9 unit crossed in front of me and pulled up next to the officer's car. The female officer reappeared and explained, "Sir, I have reason to believe that you may be possessing narcotics. I have called a K-9 unit to investigate. Would you please close the door and remain seated?" *Oh no! I'm done. That's it. My parents are going to kill me.* Thoughts of jail and handcuffs and jumpsuits filled my mind. I almost threw up.

My impaired brain held on to a glimmer of hope and I held my breath. Helplessly sitting there, I watched in the rear view mirror as the German shepherd hopped down from the SUV police vehicle. The new officer and the dog approached my car. He gave the dog a few commands and circled my car. After a quick loop, they stopped at the driver side door when the dog started barking and scratching. *Now I'm done. The dog hit!* The officer pulled the dog back, quickly instructing, "Sir, please exit the vehicle and step back to the front of the squad car." I opened the door, stepped out, and walked back to the squad car, my eyes squinting from the lights. "Hold right there. Have a seat and place your hands on the hood." Slowly sitting down, I watched as they opened the door and pulled out the bag of weed. *Damn it.* The male officer handed the bag to the female officer and turned the dog loose. The dog jumped around the vehicle, sniffing from spot to spot. *It's over. I'm toast.* My head hung in defeat. There was nothing in the vehicle except for a weed magazine, but that didn't matter, they had found a bag.

The female officer instructed, "Stand up, turn around, and place your hands behind your back." Cold cuffs tightened around my wrist. The officer turned me to face her as she explained what she had found and why I was under arrest. She also said how lucky I was. Had it been one day later, it would have been the day before my seventeenth birthday. On that day in the state of Georgia, a person is old enough to go to the Atlanta jail. But I was too high to care. She stuffed me in the back of the squad car.

Another officer arrived and they continued to search. They stripped the vehicle clean, pulling out anything from the floor mats to the change holder. They searched every piece of trash, every bag, and all through the compartments. They had no respect for my property and tossed my items around carelessly.

Thirty minutes later they finally finished. But they stood around having a conversation. Like it was the cool hangout spot. *What are they doing? Come on, come on, let's go!* I wanted to shout but knew it would go nowhere. The officer's heat was on full blast, and with my winter jacket on, I was starting to overheat. I was feeling extremely claustrophobic; there was no room to move. I couldn't move my arms or my legs and started freaking out. Another ten minutes passed and they just kept talking. I did everything I could to calm my nerves: taking deep breaths in and exhaling, focusing on a happy place, singing, but nothing was working. My chest was about to explode with anxiety.

Five more minutes passed and the K-9 officer said, "Great job, guys, well done." He gave both officers a high-five and left the scene.

A small glimmer of relief set in. *All right, here we go. I hope.* They weren't moving. Another five minutes passed and she was just talking, laughing, smiling... Finally she bid farewell and walked toward the vehicle. The door opened and as she sat down, she immediately reached to shut the heat off. *Oh WOW! Thank God. What a relief.* She turned the lights off and we drove away.

Ten minutes later, we pulled into the Alpharetta police headquarters. Large metal gates with barbed wire parted ways and we entered the facility. The officer parked the car, stepped back to my door, popped it open, and helped me wiggle out. A little calmer now that I wasn't folded up in the back seat, I remained quiet. "OK, sir, walk toward the door." She clicked on her shoulder pad radio and said, "Charlie Bravo, coming in for intake." Buzz- the large steel door popped open a few inches. Using all her weight to open the door, we stepped into a small room and waited for that door to shut before another door popped open like the first one. Stepping through the second, we walked as she held the chain between my cuffs until we reached a bland room, empty except for a table and a chair on either side. "OK, have a seat," she pointed at the blue plastic chair. Still in cuffs, I sat down.

Another male officer entered the room and chatted with the arresting officer. Seemingly in good spirits, he was cutting up and making jokes. I didn't find it very funny. Pissed off, I sat in silence. Still, I felt cool. The female officer pulled out some papers and started writing up a report. The male officer tried to spark a conversation with me, asking questions about where I go to school, how much a bag of weed goes for these days, If I like to party. He seemed harmless, but I didn't answer a single question. All of a sudden, a voice came over the female officer's radio, "Peters, you there?"

She clicked the button on her shoulder and pointed her voice into the black speaker, "Loud and clear, over."

"Aaah, the K-9 is unusually interested in the driver seat. You might want to go ahead and have him strip searched. Over."

"Ten-four."

Damn it! No! No! No! Just when I thought I had gotten away with the big stash. The male officer stood up, put on blue latex gloves, and started searching through the pockets on the outside of my coat. He pulled down the main zipper, spread it open and immediately unzipped the small zipper on the inside of the coat. Reaching in, he quickly pulled out the five rolled up bags. "Awww, you piece of shit," he turned and held up the bags.

With a stunned look, Peters stared before calmly saying, "Well, that changes things a bit. Bring them over here, please." He set the bags on the table and continued the search. There was nothing else, but he seemed satisfied. The male officer separated all five bags plus the one they found in the vehicle and laid them out. They then took all the contents out of my wallet, including fifty dollars and neatly laid them out. Peters stepped up on a chair, holding a camera, and the light flashed, freezing time. My time. Time a judge would soon see.

Officer Peters brought over the oldest scale I had ever seen, with a flat circular disk on one side, a larger one on the other side, and a bar connecting the two. She placed one bag on the larger disk and balanced out the difference. Fortunately, all the bags totaled less than an ounce. In the state of Georgia, possession of marijuana over an ounce is a felony and under an ounce is a misdemeanor.

Finally, she finished the paperwork and asked for my parents' phone number. I responded with a bit of haughtiness. "Seven seven zero, five five five, nine thousand." Fifteen minutes later my parents showed up, outraged. After the officers explained what happened, they cut me loose. I walked away holding a speeding ticket and a possession of marijuana charge. My furious parents decided to take matters into their own hands. A court date was scheduled, but my parents paid for an attorney. The attorney performed his magic and the charges were dropped. The judge required me only to perform forty community service hours and submit to two drug screens. I paid no serious consequences. A loss of a car, a short grounding, but nothing that stung enough to convince me to quit. Honestly, I wouldn't have stopped for anything.

During the next six months, I managed to stay out of trouble, but continued using despite my parents' best attempts to change my path. In my mind, I was having too much fun. The substances made life magical. The chemically-induced fog blurred reality, and reality is such a bore. Impairment was fun. Who cares if I got arrested? It won't happen again. I'm just having fun. Besides, I'm young. Everything is fun high. School is fun high. Social events are fun high. Hell, staring at a wall is fun high.

Parents think differently. No fun. Reality. What's reality? I don't know, but they keep trying to bring me there. I don't want to be there! Stop. Leave me alone. I'm fine. Shut up! Go away! Take your drug tests and shove them up your ass!

Fine! Take my car away. I don't care. You can't stop me. Fine! Drive me to school. Fine! Embarrass me. Fine! Ground me. Whatever! I hate you. Fine! I'm GONE! I'm back! Fine! This sucks! You suck! I don't care! I'm sorry! I messed up. Go away. Leave me alone. Whatever.

The battle continued with substances on one side and loving parents on the other. High versus sober, hostile versus amicable. Relentless and consistent, my parents continued to fight. Drowning in substances and refusing help, I stayed on the other side. A life-saving hand stretched out and I slapped it away, falling deeper below the surface. The hand chased and I ran farther, but it continued to follow. Annoying, nagging, bugging. Persistent and obsessive and driving me crazy. Anger exploded from all pores, building wall after wall of resentment. Now I just wanted to use to escape the nagging.

Thanksgiving break came around. During this period I was taking a high dose of an antidepressant. I had grown four inches in the last year and towered over the world. Tall, skinny, and lanky, I felt alienated, out of place, awkward. Peers were constantly reminding me by poking fun and I became extremely self-conscious. Sensing my depression, my parents took me to a psychiatrist where I was prescribed medication. It took the edge off, but I had already developed the best habit ever.

When I combined this medication with alcohol and marijuana, I felt invincible. One night at a friend's parent's party, I noticed a bottle of whiskey sitting on the snack table. Sitting innocently in the light, it was calling my name. It was seductive and irresistible and made promises of a night of fun. When no one was looking, I dumped as much whiskey as I could into a red Solo cup half-full of Coke. No one saw a thing or really even cared for that matter. Four full glasses later, I felt amazing. Life was shining and glowing. It was wonderful. No anxious feelings, no depressed thoughts, just pure bliss. Liquored up and ready for a night of fun, I left the house. It was time to get high. Not that I wasn't already high, but there's always more. I drove fifteen minutes to my old neighborhood and picked up my friend, Tyler. He hopped in my car and we drove around the neighborhood like usual, smoking a bowl. It was dark and raining heavily. Out of nowhere a sudden urge to go off-roading took over. Impulsiveness was my best friend. Quick to act, slow to think. Liquor, medication, and marijuana were in control. There was no filter, just actions.

I jerked the wheel to the left, bouncing both left wheels over the curb, splashing into the soupy mixture of grass and water— someone's front yard. Quickly jerking the wheel to the right, I bounced back onto the street. Tyler was laughing and shouting, having a ball. It was exhilarating, and I was just getting started. Driving another twenty yards, I jerked the wheel to the right, bouncing the opposite side and driving a little bit further in the grass. Proceeding down the street, I turned the front right tire into the yard of my old next door neighbor. Realizing whose yard it was, I quickly jerked the wheel back to the street, then veered to the left toward another yard, bouncing all four wheels into the yard. I drove about fifteen yards and hopped back into the street. Stopping in the middle of the street, I paused for a moment before looking over at Tyler. He was laughing uncontrollably. Numb with adrenaline, liquor, medication, and marijuana, I remained calm and waited until he caught his breath before I released the ultimate plan. "Let's go get the Jones's."

His eyes lit up, "Yeah!" The Jones's and I were constantly butting heads. They were always telling my parents and other boys' parents of our "unfit" actions.

With this in mind, I stomped on the gas. I was on a mission for revenge. Hauling down the street, I took a sharp left before jerking the wheel to the right, crossing over the Jones's driveway into the grass, mere feet from their front door. The vehicle slid through the slick yard, spraying wet grass in every direction as the mud terrain tires cut through the well-manicured yard. The Jeep bounced back over the curb, into the street, and off we went. Tyler looked over at me with a timid expression, "Damn, dude, that was fun, but I think that's enough." Agreeing with him, I drove back to his house and dropped him off.

It was getting late and time for me to retire. On the way back to my parents' neighborhood, I passed a neighborhood I just couldn't pass up. The houses were priced in the millions and the lawns received more attention than the kids. A five million dollar home with a long steep driveway sat upon a hill. On the far side of the driveway was a large grass hill with nothing but open space. Stomping on the gas, I shot over the driveway and bounced into the spongy wet yard. It felt like an ice skating rink as I slipped and slid through the yard. It only lasted seconds, but the damage would echo for months—not that I cared. I wanted more but suddenly the thought of blue police lights pierced my thoughts, so I pulled the wheel to the left and bounced back on the asphalt, still feeling rebellious. The temptation was still too strong. It was so much fun, I drove a little bit farther and hopped over yet another curb—another yard. Driving a few yards, I made my final tracks and bounced back onto the street. *OK, I'm done. That's enough. No more.* I drove back to my parents' house and parked the vehicle. Luckily, all the lights were off in the house, signaling my parents were asleep. Slowly cracking open the front door, I tiptoed up to my room and passed out in my clothes.

The next morning, I woke to the sun blaring straight through my windows. My head felt like a landmine had dropped on it. When I stood up, I lost my balance and fell back onto the bed. I was still drunk. Instead of standing, I sat on the edge of the bed and attempted to pull my brain together. *What happened last night? What did I do? Where did I go? Based on this hangover, I must have had a good time.* I continued searching for a lost memory, but nothing came to mind. Just blur, haze, fog.

Quickly giving up and attempting to aid the pain-staking hangover, I staggered to the bathroom to pull myself together. Reflecting back in the mirror was a face that revealed the toll of the substances. My eyes were bloodshot, slightly puffy, and surrounded by the usual dark bags. To cover my tracks, I dropped Visine in my eyes and brushed my teeth, eliminating the leftover taste of booze. It was the best attempt I could make to brighten a face resembling death. I changed clothes and walked downstairs to find the house empty. Both my parents were long gone to work. I was relieved, knowing I didn't have to pretend to be cheerful and not hung over. It was a constant battle to pretend that I wasn't feeling like death every morning.

Needing to fill my stomach, I opened the refrigerator in search of a container of orange juice, but found nothing. The refrigerator in the garage always had back-up so I went on a hunt. I pulled open the refrigerator door and to my delight I found a full gallon of Tropicana Orange Juice. Snatching the jug, I closed the door and turned around, freezing dead in my tracks. My eyes opened wide as fear enveloped me. Directly in front of me sat my Jeep, shining brightly in the sunlight and completely covered in grass. Large clumps and bits of mud, grass, sticks, and leaves were stuck in every nook, crevice, and crack. Dead grass littered the windows, tires and windshield wipers, and the chrome brush guard was dyed brown and yellow with bits and pieces of people's front yards.

All it took was one glance and the memory of last night slapped me in the face. My grip loosened and I dropped the gallon of orange juice as I frantically searched for a bucket. The car almost needed a pressure washer to loosen the grass, but I all I had were my hands and a sponge. I rinsed the car and started scrubbing and scrubbing and scrubbing. The sun beamed on my forehead and the combination of the heat, physical labor, and the creeping hangover almost split my head open, but eliminating the evidence was way more important. A couple hours passed before the Jeep was sparkling like new in the glistening sunlight.

With the car clean, I went back inside, ate breakfast, and pretended nothing happened. Confident I had washed away the evidence, I felt secure that no one knew a thing. My mind quickly shifted to the real problem at hand: the next high. I was desperate and needed to smoke. Knowing it would dull the pain of the splitting headache, I called Tyler. He answered, "What's up, man?"

"Wow, do you remember last night?" I was nervous.

He laughed, "Yeah, dude, that was out of control."

"Man, you're telling me. But anyways, I was wondering if we could blaze some."

"Yeah, come on over."

As I drove through the neighborhood, my jaw hit the floor. Each new track quickly replayed each joy ride. It scared me to death. *How could I have done so much damage? What was I thinking? How stupid.* The Bermuda grass that covered the yards dies in the winter. It would be five months before the damage could even begin to repair.

I pulled into Tyler's house. He ran out and jumped in the Jeep.

Anxiously I asked, "Have you seen the yards?"

He chuckled a bit before saying, "Nope."

I put the car in reverse and backed out of the driveway. We drove around the neighborhood assessing the damage in silence. It was a lot worse than we ever imagined.

Later that night, I was lying on the couch watching TV when my mom came home and listened to the messages on the answering machine. I thought nothing of it until I heard Mr. Jones's voice state, "Yes, Mr. and Mrs. Hepler, we have good evidence that last night your son drove through our lawn, narrowly missing our house. I strongly suggest you call us back before we call the police."

I peeked my eyes over the couch and saw the absolute horror on my mom's face. She practically flew over to me, clutching the phone in her right hand, and demanded, "What on earth have you done?"

"Aaaah, aah, well, you heard him."

"OH MY GOSH! Have you lost your mind? They're going to press charges."

"No, they're not. Just chill out, Mom." I tried to calm her down, but she had none of it and dialed the number. I couldn't believe it when she said we would be over immediately. *What! Are you joking?* An urgent need to escape came over me. Thoughts of weed and alcohol were dancing through my brain, promising serenity and peace, but the demanding shouts coming from my mother took center stage. I had no choice; I had to face my actions. The nerves in my chest exploded with panic. Only weed and alcohol would help. Need to get high. I zoned out and plopped into the front seat. Right as we were pulling out, my dad pulled in.

"Roll down the window, Chad, and tell him what you've done."

Not surprised, my dad climbed into the back seat. He had seen the evidence on my car that morning, but was too fed up with my constant idiotic behavior to bother confronting me for the thousandth time. It was worthless to tell me to stop. Not to mention they had tried every other form of punishment in the book. I just wanted to get messed up. That's it. Anything but sober. It took the rumbling anxious feeling out of my chest. Pure relaxation. Not a care in the world. When I was impaired, I could be sociable and actually enjoy it. Not to mention getting high was fun.

"Oh my God!" my mom whispered as we passed the lawns. "These are all yours, aren't they?"

I nodded my head, avoiding eye contact by staring out the window.

My dad chimed in, "You have really messed up this time. You're going to be lucky if you don't go to jail over this." I said nothing.

We pulled into the Jones's driveway and exited the vehicle. I knocked on the front door. My heart was beating so fast it felt like it was going to explode out of my chest. The door swung open and there stood Mr. Jones. He had a stern look, but said nothing.

I started, "Hey, Mr. Jones, I am extremely sorry about all this. I was not in a good state of mind and truly want to apologize."

Mr. Jones said nothing for what felt like an eternity. Weighted with shame, my eyes fell to the ground. I was at his mercy. Finally he responded, "Not a good thing. I don't know what to do about this. You... You... piece of... What were you doing?"

The rhetorical question drove the point home. His tone was full of rage and the look in his eyes was full of hatred. Steam was practically flowing from his ears and his face was bright red.

"Look." He pointed at the distance between the house and the tracks. "Look at how close you were to my home. My entire family lives here. You could have killed us all!"

I frantically searched my brain for something to say, but guilt and shame piled to an unbearable weight. Reality sunk in deep. Reality is such a stranger. With my eyes still focused at his feet, I made my best attempt to rectify my actions. "I would like to help repair the grass and also want to offer to take care of your yard for however long you'd like."

"No, Chad, I enjoy taking care of my lawn. The only thing I want is to never see you in this neighborhood again. And if you do come back, you better believe I will be calling the police."

"Yes, sir." There was nothing else I could say. With my head still drooping, I tried to swallow the knot in my throat and walked back to the vehicle where my parents stood waiting. "OK, let's go," I muttered and stepped back into the vehicle.

My parents continued to punish me, taking away privilege after privilege, dragging me to drug counselors and forcing me to perform hours of yard work. Nothing took away the drive to get high or drunk. It was my best friend. It didn't yell at me. It didn't judge me. It didn't cause pain. It just soothed. Escaped. Comforted. No problems. Relaxation. Fun. Fun. Fun.

A month later, I was lying in bed on a Wednesday night when I got a phone call from one of the girls in the neighborhood across the street. Bubbly and excited, she exclaimed, "Hey, honey, it's Wednesday night. You know what that means, don't you?"

"Aaah, no, not really. What's up?"

"It's hump day! Me and Karen are drinking, you better come hang out."

"Yeah, definitely. Can you come pick me up in an hour?"

"Sure thing, cutie. Call me when you're ready."

"Yes, ma'am." Hanging up the phone, I snuck down the hallway to see if my parents' light was on. It was, but they were in their room winding down. Only a few moments later and I would be off in to my favorite place- impairment. A strong feeling of excitement surged through my brain just thinking about being drunk. Wide awake with excitement, I went back to my room and started taking shots of warm cheap vodka stashed in a water bottle underneath my bed.

The hour passed as slow as molasses, but once that light clicked off I knew I was in the clear. The shots of vodka had passed through my stomach and straight into my bloodstream, creating the euphoric feeling of impairment. A smile crossed my face. The world shimmered and the constant anxious feeling was drowning. I jumped on the phone and the girls headed over. It was rainy and cold, but I was buzzed and ready for a fun night.

Reaching down to the handle of the silver Honda Accord, I pulled it open and jumped in the backseat. Both girls smiled at me. From the passenger seat, Karen asked, "What's up, darling?"

"What's up, girls, what's going on?"

With a giant smile, Karen held up a cheap bottle of flavored rum and said, "Just having a little fun."

"Hell, yeah, let me see that." I grabbed the bottle, popped the top, and took a giant swig. The warm peach-flavored rum flowed down my throat, creating an urge to gag, but it quickly passed and the comforting, warming sensation tingled all the way down. Shaking my head, I let out a "Whew!" and handed the bottle back. "So what's the plan?"

Jessica, the driver, responded, "Well, Karen's parents aren't asleep yet, so we have to go over there for a few minutes." I shot Karen a look of pure anger as the thought of waiting to drink sent panic through my chest. "Don't worry, I'm gonna let you drive my car until we can come back out."

"Cool, that'll work." We drove over to Karen's house. The girls hopped out and I jumped in the driver's seat. Cranking up the music, I zoomed off with the bottle of rum stuck between my legs. Every couple of minutes I took a swig as I veered around the sharp turns. The more sips I took, the braver I became. Driving the vehicle went from a leisurely cruise to an aggressive Indy-style race. The provoking hairpin turns became an obstacle course that offered excitement and thrills. All of a sudden, from around a corner, I came face to face with headlights. The bright lights blinded me and the sound of the horn shook my nerves. Squinting with fear, I jerked the wheel to the left, crossing in front of the vehicle. After barely dodging it, I slammed on the brakes and my car went into a dead slide. The steering wheel locked up and I held on for my life. The front left tire slammed the curb, propelling the entire car up into the air before landing in someone's front yard. My head bounced back and forth from the impact and my arms flailed through the air. After quickly collecting my thoughts, I realized I was fine, but I panicked about the other vehicle. I glanced in the rear view mirror to see. The red brake lights were lighting up the street. *Oh shit oh shit oh shit! I'm getting a DUI. Do something!* I tossed the bottle under the passenger seat, slammed the stick in reverse and stomped the gas. I could only pray the wheels would catch and pull me out of the yard. If a tow truck came, I was done. Police would show, the car would be towed, the owners would sue, and I would sit in jail. *Please, please, please reverse. Yes!* The car bounced, scraped and slid, rolling back into the street. Relief washed over me, but what was the other car doing? I paused, holding my breath, just staring in the rearview mirror. *Please just drive. Please just go away.* Seconds passed, the brake lights switched off and the other car drove away. *Thank God!* Immediately hopping out into the cold rain, I assessed the damage. *OH NO! OH CRAP! THAT'S BAD!* The left front tire was flat, slammed into the fender, and the bumper had a dent the size of a human head. *Holy cow! WHAT do I do? What do I do?* I tried to pull my brain for answers. Fear, anxiety, and booze clouded everything. *I'll just fix the flat. That'll work. YEAH! At least I can drive the car back to the house.* Jumping back in the car, I dialed Jessica. She answered, "Hello."

"Aaah, haaay Jessica, your car got a flat and I'm trying to figure out where the jack is."

Her voice exploded with fear, "What? Are you serious? Where are you?"

"Aaah, I'm not far from Karen's. I might just be able to make it back there."

"OK, do that."

"All right, bye." Realizing I had to fix the flat, I hopped back into the rain, searching frantically through the trunk for the jack. I found nothing. The car was in the middle of the street and I had to do something. Any second now, someone was bound to drive by. I knew I smelled like booze and was in no condition to talk to anyone.

Accepting the damage was much more than just the flat tire, I jumped back in the driver's seat, shifted the car into gear, and attempted to move. The wheel bounced, shook, and ground against the fender. The dash vibrated, the steering wheel twisted uncontrollably left and right, but the car was moving. Relieved, I knew I could work my way back to the house. Three miles per hour was better than zero miles per hour.

The car stalled right as I pulled up to the edge of the driveway. I made it, but I immediately came face to face with Karen and Jessica, arms crossed and furious. Like a scared puppy, I cautiously stepped out of the vehicle. Looking back at the car, I saw half of the bumper lying on the ground. Jessica took one glance at her car and just started bawling. Karen held her while she cried. I felt terrible. *Ohh man... I'm such a jerk.* Minutes passed as Jessica continued to cry. Through her weeps she sobbed, "I don't know what to do. I can't tell my dad. I can't tell my dad that." More cries and sobs. "I can't tell my dad someone else was driving."

I had to help. "Yes, you can. I will take the blame. You didn't do anything wrong."

Jessica started bawling again. Infuriated, Karen pointed down the street and demanded, "Leave, Chad. Just go home." Filled with guilt, I slowly turned my back to them and proceeded down the sidewalk. I never heard from Jessica or Karen again.

A few weeks later I was out of school for Christmas break. Another great excuse to be drinking. Not that I ever ran out of excuses, but at Christmas time it was a given. Drinking and hanging out with friends and not going to school was a dream. We went driving and drinking. Again. By this point I had acquired a very real-looking fake I.D. and had no problem purchasing booze. My friend Jamie and I killed a bottle of Captain Morgan's Spiced Rum in an hour and decided to go for round two. The next bottle took a little bit longer to finish, but we had no problem accomplishing the task. Absolutely obliterated, we drove from hangout spot to hangout spot—accomplishing nothing. After a few hours, I dropped Jamie off at his house. The drive home was another drunk game to avoid the cops. To this day I am amazed that I never got pulled over. I can't count the number of times I drove intoxicated or rode with someone intoxicated.

The next morning I woke up with the usual staggering hangover. I went through the routine of piecing myself back together and walked downstairs, pretending to be just fine and not feeling like death. Stepping down the wooden stairs, I glanced over the railing to see my mom in the dining room, hanging Christmas decorations. She set a little Santa Claus figurine on a shelf before giving me a disgusted look. The look told it all, but I couldn't remember a thing. *What'd I do? What'd I do? What happened?* I searched my brain, but nothing came to mind. Instead, I pretended to be just fine.

Cheerfully I greeted her, "Oh, hey Mom." She didn't say a word and went back to her decorations. Walking over to her, I fearfully asked, "What's wrong?"

Looking up with an expression of complete shock, she asked with a strained voice, "Oh my God, you don't remember, do you?"

I tried to play back the night before. Still just blankness, nothing, not even a hint. I played it safe by lying, "Sure I do. What's the matter?"

With the same look of disgust, she responded, "You have some apologizing to do to your father, son."

OH RIGHT! A blurry image sparked through my brain. Bits and pieces were there, trying desperately to connect. All I could really picture was yelling, screaming, and cursing. But nothing else. No motives. No reasons. Just anger.

Going down to the basement to search for my dad, I found him tinkering in the workroom. Before saying anything, I prepared myself for the usual conversation of how I need to quit drinking and get myself together. He must have felt my presence because he turned and glanced over his shoulder. Quietly and calmly he addressed me, "Oh, hi Chad." Then he went back to his tinkering.

"Hey Dad, umm... Well... I wanted to apologize for last night."

He didn't respond, just kept tinkering. *What did I do? Why isn't he talking?* Confused, I searched my brain for something else to say. I came out with the usual next day comment. A comment full of lies and empty promises. "I won't do it again. I'm gonna change."

He kept working, saying nothing, so I turned to leave the room. *What on earth? What's going on? That was really weird.* Normally we would have a talk and he would tell me what all I did wrong and how I needed to change. *Maybe he's fed up and has simply given up on me. Sweet! That'd be awesome! Did I break them? I think so!* Relief fell over me and I envisioned getting drunk and high whenever I wanted.

Life Story

DING DONG. DING DONG. My thoughts were broken by a loud bell noise. Bolting upright in bed, I tried to figure out what was going on. The guys in the cabin were putting on their shoes, tying their laces, putting on overcoats and filing out the screen door. Fritz came walking from around the corner of the bathroom, looked up, and said, "Come on, man, it's dinner time." *Dinner! Food! I love food.* A small glimmer of joy fluttered through my stomach, but was snuffed by the reminder of being in rehab. Jumping down from the bed, I threw on the blue winter coat and shuffled out the door.

Stepping carefully, I followed the guys to the dining hall. As soon as I swung back the wooden door, the smell of steak smacked me in the face. *Mmm, that smells delicious.* Five picnic benches stretched in a straight line for thirty feet. A few feet from the end was a wall with familiar wood paneling, but on either side was an open doorframe. The guys were lining up on the left side. Joining the line, I could feel the curious looks. Finally, the guy in front of me asked, "Hey, what's your name?" Shaking my hand, he declared, "I'm Germ." He stood about six feet tall, with a slim frame, light blond/orange surfer hair, some freckles, and high cheekbones. A few guys were poking fun at him, but I didn't pay much attention. Shaking a few more hands, I felt more comfortable and patiently waited until we were allowed into the kitchen.

A few counselors went ahead of us, but once they were seated with trays of food, we were granted access. I crossed under the doorframe and was shocked at the amount of delicious food sitting on the mobile stainless steel countertops. There were steaks, potatoes, gravy, corn, fresh fruit, vegetables, and two pans of warm brownies. I looked at Germ on the other side of the buffet line and exclaimed, "Man, this is great."

He looked up, "Yeah, at least they feed us good, right?"

Taking at least one serving of each bowl, I filled my plastic tray and sat down. It was only minutes later before I was rubbing my stomach and looking down at a clear plate. "What a meal," I said to the guy next to me. He had a mouth full of food, but nodded in agreement. Once he finished chewing, he introduced himself, "What's up, dude, I'm Chris." I had seen him earlier in line. He was a shorter guy, but well-built with short, dark hair and blue eyes. His round face contained a few red blemishes on his cheeks. He had a sense of arrogance to him.

Sitting there for a few minutes, I tried to figure out what to do next. Noticing a few guys getting up with a clear tray, I followed them back into the kitchen and tossed my tray in a large steel sink. As I walked out of the kitchen, I noticed a piece of paper tacked on the wall with names and dates written on it. The top of the sheet read "Kitchen Duties." Going back to my seat I asked Chris, "Hey man, what's up with that kitchen duties sheet?"

He shoveled a spoon full of potatoes into his mouth before attempting to explain, "Every week," he paused and took a swig of Kool-Aid from a plastic red cup before starting again. "Every week three different guys have to help with the food prep and cleanup after each meal. It's not too bad except for in the morning you have to wake up thirty minutes earlier."

"Hmm." I thought for a moment before asking, "What time do we wake up?"

His expression turned sour as he responded, "Six thirty."

During the next twenty minutes, people finished eating and hung around the porch or the side tables. Three guys were wiping down tables, sweeping the floor, and preparing a mop bucket. All of a sudden, an older man with balding gray hair walked through the door holding a cardboard box. A couple guys noticed the man and exclaimed, "Willie!" Ignoring them, he hobbled to the far table. Through his Coke-bottle glasses, he peered down at the box and pulled out an assortment of envelopes. Using a pocketknife, he slit open each envelope and searched through the contents until he was satisfied. Assuming it was mail call, I sat there hoping that maybe I got a piece of mail—an unrealistic thought, considering I had only been there for a few hours, but then again, my now-crumbled box of stuff seemed to appear from nowhere. Ten minutes later, after calling excited patients to the front, Willie closed the box and walked out. We filed out and went back to the cabins. No mail for me.

After a while, I noticed some guys lining up in front of a small shack between cabin 2 and cabin 3. Nudging Fritz, I asked "What are they doing?"

"Lockers!"

"What? I don't get it."

Full of excitement he explained, "Lockers are where we keep personal items that we can't have regular access to. Like razors, shaving cream, workout equipment, candy bars, snacks, cigarettes, or whatever. You know, all the good stuff. The stuff us addicts and alcoholics can't keep on our own."

Addicts and alcoholics? I'm not an addict or alcoholic! This is so stupid. Where the hell am I?

The process took about forty-five minutes, and once they finished, the boys lined up where Carsten had told me not to cross the gap in the fence. Joining the line, I learned we were going into the building for a movie.

When the movie finished, the light flicked on and everyone formed a circle with the blue plastic chairs. *What is going on?* It was a whole new concept to me. Apparently it was an alcoholics recovery meeting. *I'm not an alcoholic! Get me out of here!* I wanted to leave, but I knew that would turn out bad. Instead, I closed my mind and tried to tune it out. The meeting started with a reading from some recovery book. Different guys read different sections, but I didn't pay any attention, and besides, the things they were talking about were almost in a different language. I was still in a complete state of shock.

The guys went around the circle introducing themselves as an alcoholic or addict and talking about who-knows-what. Not having anything to say, I attempted to pass, but the guy in charge asked me to say something. Refusing to introduce myself as an alcoholic, I simply said my name. Not sure what else to talk about, I explained my fight with the escorters. Telling the story brought back the anger and inflated my resentments to a new level. *What the hell? I don't need this! I'm fine. This is so stupid.*

Finally, after a full hour, the meeting ended. Everyone stood up with their arms around each other's shoulders. I didn't know what to do and tried to walk away. Fritz released his hold, creating a hole in the circle, and said, "Come on, dude, get in here." Trying to politely decline, I shook my head, but everyone joined in and I couldn't resist. It felt good to at least be part of the group, but they all started chanting a recovery prayer.

As we were walking out of the building, I asked Germ what we were doing now. With a smile he said, "Free time, whatever you want. Well, not whatever, but come on, follow me." There was a path carved in the snow that headed toward a dark shack. It leaned sideways with scrap pieces of board stuck all over it and a small black tube jutting from the roof. It looked like a place to kill people or something.

The wooden porch creaked and cracked as I followed Germ over the rotting boards toward the large half-hung door that didn't fully close. Crossing under the doorframe, I entered the room—surprised to find what the building held. In the middle of the shed, taking up most of the space, was a ping pong table. Next to that were an old dusty foosball table and a stove-style fireplace. On the opposite side was a set of weights. The weights were old and rusty, but nonetheless it was comforting to see something that I enjoyed doing.

The room was frigid, just as cold as the outside, but the freshly lit fire offered warmth. Sitting by the fire, I watched the intense game of ping pong unfolding directly in front of me and thought more about where I was. It pissed me off. My anger toward my parents escalated again. *How could they do this? My life... My perfect life. They are messing it all up. How dare they. To me... Their son. This is what I get? I don't deserve this.*

My thoughts were going nowhere in circles of anger and resentments. They were toxic, but the weight set offered an escape. Standing up, I began fidgeting with the rusty weights and started lifting. My anger fueled my muscles. Images of destruction filled my brain. It helped, and I wore myself out.

Eleven thirty came around and we retired to the cabins. I brushed my teeth, washed my face, took out my contacts, climbed up the bunk bed, and settled under the warm covers. Exhausted from the overly intense day, I closed my eyes and started praying that when I woke up, this would all be a dream and I'd be sprawled in my own bed at home.

Disappointment sank in the next morning when I awoke to the noise of someone clapping and chanting. Rubbing my sticky eyes, I rolled over toward the sound. It was Carsten standing in the doorway with an idiotic smile. The next thing I knew, the fluorescent white light bulbs illuminated right above my bed, demanding my presence. Flopping back to the other side, I tried to pretend this wasn't happening. *Go away! Such garbage. It's still dark out!*

A few minutes passed before I finally forced myself to wake up and slid off the bed, dropping about a foot. Washing my face, brushing my teeth, and putting in my contacts, I faced the morning as best I could. Knowing the temperature outside would be frigid, I bundled up before walking to breakfast. On the way, I passed a giant thermometer that had to be broken. It read zero degrees. In disbelief, I hit the guy next to me and asked, "Is that real?"

"Sure is, man. Watch this." He spit on the sidewalk, then rubbed it with his shoe. The spit didn't smear. Amazingly, in the time that the spit hit the ground until the time he rubbed it, it had already frozen. I couldn't believe it. I knew it was cold, but I had never experienced zero degrees before.

After breakfast, we went over to the same building where the movie had been shown. The Treatment House. We gathered in another circle, which seemed odd, but whatever. One of the guys read a daily devotional from another recovery book. After it was read, each person was required to reflect upon it. I offered some half-hearted statement before wrapping our arms around one another's shoulder. *There goes that prayer thing again. What is this garbage? Blah. Blah. Blah. So stupid. Get me out of here. I don't have a problem.*

We broke up and spilled outside where Carsten and a few other counselors were standing. Each held a yellow sticky note and quickly read off different names. Carsten called my name along with a couple others, and we followed him into a tiny workshop. The floor was cement and the walls were covered with all types of tools dangling on long rusty nails. The room was frigid, maybe even colder than outside, but Carsten quickly ripped up some pieces of newspaper, threw them in the furnace, and tossed in a few logs. A couple minutes later a warm, comforting fire was roaring. "All right," he said as he started fidgeting with a few tools. "You guys are lucky because for the whole day today we are going to be in this room where it's warm, building bunk beds from that pile of logs." He pointed at a pile of shaven six-foot logs.

Lucky, I don't think so! More like unlucky! He assigned each guy a different task and we went to work. My task was to shave down the ends of a smaller set of logs with a little motorized grinder. I sat there grinding down the ends while Carsten took a large drill called a Boar Hogger and drilled holes into the thicker logs. A couple guys were shaving more logs and one younger guy was not really doing anything. Finally, Carsten noticed the boy's lack of involvement and sarcastically asked, "Thomas, you, aaah, getting a lot done over there?" From the floor, Thomas looked up and rolled his eyes before tinkering with a hammer on a piece of wood. Thomas couldn't have been any older than fourteen. He was very short, with long fro-like curly hair and blue eyes. Ugly boomerang-shaped light blue earrings hung from his ears. In a matter of seconds, Carsten's expression went from slightly annoyed to irritated.

"Thomas! What are you doing?"

From the dusty cement floor, Thomas rolled his eyes again and said, "Whaaaat, man, I'm working. Leave me alone." This time he grabbed a nail and started hammering it into a piece of scrap wood. At the sad attempt at construction, Carsten became more amused than angry and gave Thomas direction, while we all went back to work. The day dragged on and on and my mind began wandering.

The smell of the burning logs, mixed with the piney cold air, fluttered memories through my mind. It reminded me of Park City, Utah. The memory was relaxing and I let my mind escape. I dreamed I was there. Anywhere but here was nice, and Park City memories held nothing but happiness. The most recent trip was the most exciting.

I was back on my last spring break during my junior year of high school. A few days before I left, I called up my dealer— knowing nothing would make the trip better than a bag of weed and a few pills. The pills were for the plane ride and the weed, well, was for the mountains, of course. I mean, what could be better than getting stoned and skiing down a mountain? Not sure how to get the weed through the airport, I began researching different ideas. I searched the Internet, called a couple friends, and asked my dealer. The consensus came down to six plastic baggies, peanut butter, rubber bands and duct tape. Knowing the airport security would be tight, with 9/11 only a few years back, I didn't take any risks. First I placed the weed in one baggie, rolled it up, and repeated the process with a second and third baggie. I rolled the three baggies as one and rubber banded it closed. Taking a spoonful of peanut butter, I rubbed a heaping amount all over the rolled bags, which apparently would conceal the smell from any nosey canines. In hindsight, it seems pretty dumb, but to a mind full of THC and other chemicals, it was ingenious. I was outsmarting the airport, or so I hoped.

After the peanut butter came three more baggies and a final rubber band. My nose couldn't smell a thing. It was perfect, so clever, and the smirk ran across my face. It was exciting, knowing the danger I was about to face. I craved danger. Another piece to my addictive brain. Danger. Adrenaline. The two go hand in hand to create a different high. Another high. It all feels good. Adrenaline calmed me down, or maybe it just blocked out the anxiety. Not sure, but it felt good. The final step was to duct tape the bag along with a brand new glass pipe to my inner thigh. Surely no one would search there.

Walking through the airport, my mind began racing with worry, adrenaline, and excitement. A tall man dressed in military uniform held a German shepherd on a tight leash. They were coming my way. My throat tightened and my legs went numb. The anxiety took control. I stared as he approached, but quickly darted my eyes. *Don't look at him. Don't give him a reason.* Inside I panicked, but outside I remained cool and calm. Only my peripheral vision followed him. Images of jail, handcuffs, and courtrooms saturated my thoughts. *He knows. He has to know. This is it. I'm done.* The man held his stare straight forward, but the dog's glare seemed to be focused on my leg. I couldn't breathe. The anxiety constricted every muscle. The dog strolled by. No bark. No scratch. No whimper. He just kept walking. My chest relaxed, the anxiety released, and the dog continued in stride. They were behind me still walking. I couldn't take it anymore. Impairment was calling my name. Ten feet to the right was a sign for the bathroom, so I peeled off from the group and locked myself in the stall. My hand reached for the two white Xanax bars and popped them into my mouth. Just knowing a substance was in my body, a sense of calm enveloped me. As far as I was concerned, I was in the clear. I had won. I escaped the airport security and managed to smuggle drugs through the airport. So clever.

Three hours passed before it was time to eat lunch. After lunch we had an hour of free time, and I decided to try my luck in the ping pong matches. I was terrible, but hoped that after two months I would look like one of the guys on late night ESPN channels.

Before going back to work, one of the counselors brought out a box of orange-cream ice cream bars. They were tasty and let my brain escape in the flavors. We worked until four thirty and then we went back to the cabins.

Sitting on the edge of the lower bunk, untying my boots, two guys walked in covered in dirt and a foul stench, complaining about how they had to shovel horse and cow poop all day. I decided not to tell them that I sat around in a warm, clean shed.

A shower and a set of fresh clothes later, I felt much better and was ready for another fulfilling dinner. As I stepped up to grab the wooden handle of the dining hall door, I noticed a piece of paper taped on the door with five names on in it. *Another list. I wonder what this could be.* We all stood patiently in line, waiting for the counselors to get their food before serving ourselves. This time we had homemade fried chicken with fresh salad, fruit, baked potatoes, green beans, and warm cookies. I sat down next to Germ and learned a little bit more about him. He was from Wayzata, Minnesota, and explained he had attended another rehab before in the city, but it clearly didn't help too much. His drug of choice was Ecstasy, which made sense because he was always dancing around like he was at some rave or something. Germ was easy to talk to and I felt like I was making a friend. This was comforting, especially in an unknown environment.

Once we finished eating, I pointed toward the front door and asked him, "So what's up with that list of names taped on the door."

His face showed excitement and he explained, "Dude, that's the list of the people who get to go to in-town meetings."

"In-town meetings?"

"Yeah, you get to ride in a Suburban to the recovery meetings and actually listen to music."

I didn't get it. I mean, get to listen to music? How exciting could that be? Apparently I hadn't been deprived long enough.

Minutes later Willie walked in with the cardboard box and went through the mail call routine. Let down again, I just kept wishing someone would send me something. Sure, I had only been there a day, but I needed something. Everyone else just seemed so happy with mail call, but I had nothing.

Willie left the room, and everyone hung out awhile on the porch. We then took thirty minutes in the cabin before heading to the Treatment House for another recovery meeting. Once again I attempted to pass on speaking, but I was forced to say something. I simply talked about the day. *This recovery stuff is dumb. Just explain to the counselors you don't need to be here. Do something. This isn't for you.*

I was starting to remember the first part of the closing prayer, but definitely didn't recite any of it. I only knew it because I had heard seemingly a thousand times already.

I started to leave the building, assuming it was free time, but Germ explained that on Saturdays and Sundays we were able to make phone calls. This was the first thing that actually lifted my spirits. *Hmmm...Phone calls... Who should I call? Should I call Jamie or my brother? Naah. I need to call Coach.* Coach Holiday was a good ol' southern boy from South Georgia who had mentored me and coached me since eighth grade. He cared for me and I had a deep respect for him, especially since he was always there to guide me as I went through many different situations on and off the track. As I dialed his number, an anxious but excited feeling surged through my body.

"Yellow."

"Coach!"

"Well, I'll be darned. How are ya, son?"

"I'm all right. Do you know where I am?"

"Oh yes, your parents have filled me in on everything, and I'm proud of ya and know this will not be any issue for you."

I let out a little sigh and replied, "Yeah, I'm a little confused and shaken up, but I'll be all right."

"Of course you will, Chad. My only regret is that I didn't really know what was going on, otherwise I would have done whatever I could to help prevent this."

"I know, I guess I was pretty good at hiding everything, huh?"

"You got that right, but we'll get through this. And make sure you do whatever you can out there to improve your life. This is nothing to be embarrassed about."

Immediately, relief and courage rolled over me. His words were always so powerful and he always said the perfect thing—whether he knew it or not. Encouragement was the only thing I needed and he nailed it. No surprise, though. That's why he was my coach. No matter what, he always spoke positively, especially during my most recent track season. It was the regional meet, the biggest meet of the regular season. Only the top two advance to the state meet. The competition was stiff with four guys jumping the same height. Coach pulled me aside. His expression was serious but calm, and his circular farm-boy hat blocked the beaming sun. Soaking in every word, I stared straight at him. "Look here, this is your meet, your time, your moment. These guys have nothing on you. This is what it's all about. This height is easy, just clear it and you're the champion."

"Next up, Hepler." The fat man in a white collared shirt demanded my jump.

Focused and psyched, I pulled the fourteen-foot pole into the air at the end of the strip of rubber track. My senses went tunneled. Only the metal box thirty yards ahead called my name. I heard nothing, smelled nothing, tasted nothing. Only in sports did the anxious feeling work to my advantage. Pressure was my best friend and the anxiety fueled my performance.

This height is easy, just clear it and you're the champion. His words echoed through my brain. *Champion. Champion. Champion. Easy. It's easy. Your moment. Your time. Your time.*

With that, I jumped into a sprint. Running, running, running. The pole balanced ten feet in the air leading the way. In one split second, my wrists lowered the bar before curling it to my shoulders and pressing toward the sky. The rubber end of the pole met the metal box, and with pure strength, my arms flexed to hold on and simultaneously jump off the ground, driving my right knee forward but leaving my left straight. The bar bent ninety degrees. The forward motion held the bar bent for a fraction of a second as I swung my left leg to catch up with the right in a motion like punting a football. The motion turned me on my back and I hung in the air with both knees pulled in to my chest. The only thing in sight was the clouds. I waited as the bar quickly straightened pulling me higher, higher, higher. Close to being completely straight, I pulled on the bar and pushed my feet toward the sky. My body was inverted twelve feet above the ground and I twisted from the hips, rotating to the left. Releasing my grip, I soared, soared, soared, staring at the ground. Gravity started to catch up. As I reached the peak, I sucked in my stomach, kicked my legs and threw my arms over my head. The bar was below me. My legs flew over, my stomach skimmed by and I almost kissed the bar as I arched my head back. The motion sent me twirling onto my back. The sky was back in sight and I fell and fell and fell. With a comfortable *thud*, my body sank deep into the mat, but the only thing that mattered was the bar. Immediately looking up, I held my breath, just staring. It didn't move. It was sitting motionless thirteen feet in the air. I had done it! The bystanders erupted with yells, cheers, and claps. Endorphins swarmed my brain. Coach was ecstatic. Jumping off the mat, I ran to him. He threw me a high five. "YEAH, BOY, YEAH. I knew it! I knew you had it in you."

I couldn't stop smiling. He pointed over at a news reporter with a three-foot camera sitting on a tripod. "Look there, son. He snapped several pictures. You're gonna be in the paper."

"Really?"

"Of course! You just won regionals and broke the school record. With that first place finish, your team should also have enough points to win the entire meet."

Pride swelled in my chest. That's right. I won and helped the team win. What a high. What a rush. Was this the feeling I aimed to find with drugs and alcohol? Maybe, but one thing was sure, it felt better than anything in the world. No substance could compare to this natural high.

Sure enough, the first thing I did the next day was check the gas station for the local paper. Flying across the top of the front page was a colored picture of me skimming over the bar. Turning to the sports section I found a colored six-inch by eight-inch picture. It was beautiful. The caption below read, "Hepler takes regional, breaking the school record, clearing thirteen feet, four inches." Another real high, not a fake one. Not induced, but created, and it was glorious. There was no need to smoke before school that day.

A higher power? Absolutely. I never pole vaulted impaired. I couldn't. It just didn't work. Pole vaulting kept me from using. Well, part of the time.

Coach Holiday's constant words of encouragement kept me going. He was a true blessing. Without those statements, I would have had nothing. Every time he talked, I soaked in every bit. For the next fifteen minutes, I listened to Coach. He flooded my head with encouragement before I replaced the phone back on the receiver and walked out into the cold. For the first time since I had arrived, my head was held high.

The next morning I woke to find the room full of sunshine. Noticing everyone still nestled in bed, I became confused. *Did I miss breakfast?* It was late. We never woke up after the sun rose. Confused and nervous, I sat up and tried to make sense of things. A few moments later, a counselor named Bill came walking in with an unusual amount of excitement. "Rise and shine, boys! Time to face a day of sobriety and, boy, is it sweet." His voice filled the room and his clapping hands startled me. I realized it was Sunday. I guessed we were allowed to sleep in, so immediately I calmed down.

Thirty-something and balding already, Bill was about six feet, one inch tall and a little overweight. I had met him once and he seemed like a decent guy, so I respected his command and dropped out of the bunk. At breakfast we had the best French toast I had ever tasted along with some fresh fruit and sausage. The sweet cinnamon mixed with maple syrup tingled my taste buds and took me back to Saturday mornings at home with my neighborhood friends.

Breakfast ended and Bill sent us back to the cabin, instructing us to wear something warm and to meet out in the field right in front of the cabins. The guys assembling in the field were far less than athletic-looking. I mean, they were even smoking cigarettes. Shuffling around in a foot of snow, we waited until a young guy named Wilder Andy came walking out with a couple of soccer balls. Andy was short with dark short hair, a big smile, large lips, and a goofy personality. His role at the facility was to run the recreational days and to go on trips because he was an expert in outdoor survival.

Andy split us up into two teams and set out some orange cones to designate boundaries and goals. It was the hardest game of soccer I had ever played. Stomping around in a foot of snow wore me out in a matter of minutes. Thirty minutes into the game, a different counselor named Tim called me over and had me follow him to his office in the Treatment House. Sitting in the cloth chair next to his desk, I watched as he pulled out a couple booklets with a few sheets that resembled a Scantron sheet. "OK, Chad, this is a series of questions that is going to go through your drug history and other personal areas. You need to be completely honest and accurate with every question. No funny business." He slid the booklets across the desk and handed me a pencil. I nodded my head and he exited the room. *Great. This is going to suck. But this is my chance. My chance to show them I don't have a problem. My chance to show them I don't need to be here. My chance to go home!*

After peeling back the front page, I read the first question: "How old where you when you first used alcohol?" The sheet gave five answers and I circled the corresponding one. The next question asked: "Out of these drugs, check the ones you have used at least once: Alcohol, Marijuana, Barbiturates, GHB, Methamphetamines, Amphetamines, and Cocaine." Fear crept over me. I stumbled with what to do. Sitting back in my chair I began debating. *Do I lie or be honest?* I had done every one on the list. But I was too afraid that if I answered truthfully I might be here longer. *If I can only show them I don't need to be here, then surely I can go home.* My mind came to a conclusion. The pencil seemed to move on its own. I checked marijuana, alcohol, and amphetamines, and moved on. Hours passed before completing the test. Upon finishing, I searched for Tim and found him in one of the counseling rooms. With a bit of nervousness I announced, "All done," and handed him the booklets with the pencil. I had lied on about half of the questions.

"All right," he stood up holding the booklets down by his side. He paused, then looked right at me to make sure I was listening. "Tonight after the recovery meeting, you are going to give your life story."

With a confused look, I said, "Life story?"

He continued, "You need to tell your story from the beginning to the present, starting with your birth all the way through your complete drug history."

"Aaah, OK." Shocked and confused, I wanted to resist, but I knew it would be a long shot. I remained quiet, but my mind panicked. *Why do I need to do a life story? Those tests will surely show I don't have a problem. I'm fine. Let me go home. This is pointless.*

"Well, we are done here. Go ahead and join the group."

Frustrated and angry, I stormed out. The game was still going on, so I was forced to join back in. Running and playing helped a little bit, but the anger stayed and the games dragged on and on.

Dinner came and went, and we were sent back to the cabin until the recovery meeting. Fritz told me that on Sunday nights some "Super Sober Guy" came to lead the meeting in the dining area. *Wonderful,* I thought. *Just what I need, an audience for my life story.*

During the meeting, my mind attempted to recreate the different stories I was going to tell. Realizing that I probably wasn't going to be sent home, I decided to tell mostly everything. Besides, it's always easier not to lie. At least, when you're telling the truth, you don't have to make up different things and try to keep them all in line. Before I went up to tell my story I thought about the first time I tried amphetamines or Adderall.

The summer before ninth grade was my time to experiment. Already experimenting with marijuana, I was open to any substance placed in front of me. One of the neighborhood boy's brothers was prescribed Adderall. I didn't know anything about it, but I became curious when a hand holding several blue and pink roundish pills stretched my way. Not really caring about the danger of the drug, I grabbed two of the pink pills and swallowed them. My friend threw back three of the blue ones and we waited. An hour later, the pills kicked in and my legs went numb with a feeling of euphoria. The feeling crawled up my legs and covered the rest of my body. What a high. The world went into high definition and everything felt beautiful. I couldn't stop talking. Without the pills, I would have never been saying the things I said. There so many emotions, so much love, so much high. I loved the grass, I loved the trees, I loved the birds, I loved myself, and I loved you. We debated what to do. Well, not so much debate, but more of a concern for how the other guy felt. Whatever you want. No, whatever you want, man. I'll do anything.

My mind was numb with complete elation. I could be sitting in a jail cell and still be the happiest boy alive. What a drug. It was the most intense feeling I had ever experienced. We started walking. The sun was shining, the summer air was warm, and the world was smiling. We walked and walked and talked and talked until clumps of dried spit stuck in the corners of our lips. Life was wonderful and nothing bothered me. The anxious rumbling feeling in my chest was numb. Hours passed but the feeling stayed. It never seemed to dissipate.

Eight hours of a pure high passed before the earth came back in sight. The come-down was hard, intense, and depressing. A feeling that good comes with a heavy price, and my mind slipped into a deep state of depression. Sad and gloomy, I just wanted to sleep, but my mind raced. *Sleep. Sleep. I need sleep.* It was one in the morning, my body was exhausted and depression flooded my mind. Four more hours passed. Flopping, squirming, and twisting, I tried everything— every position, every thought, but nothing worked. My mind squirmed. *Why can't I sleep? I took those pills twelve hours ago! All I want is sleep.* Five in the morning ticked over and the sun was rising. My brain tingled with depression. Another hour passed, the world was awake and so was I. I had a few beers stuffed under the bed and decided to polish them off, hoping they would knock me out. Thirty minutes passed before my brain relaxed. It went blank, and off I went, finally, into a dead, dreamless sleep. Not restful sleep, but something. It wasn't until four in the afternoon that my eyes finally opened. I felt terrible, crappy and sad. Swearing off Adderall forever, I got up and ate lunch. That would not be the last time, though. For whatever reason, my mind always forgot the negative side effects and totally embraced the high. Adderall became a drug to do every couple of months, usually before school. High on Adderall was the best. I could talk to anyone. Nothing scared me and it was wonderful. I felt cool and rebellious. Rebellion helped my self-esteem.

The meeting ended, and the Super Sober Guy gave me the floor. After nervously getting up, I worked my way toward the front. Before speaking I looked down, shuffling my feet as I collected my thoughts. The nervousness increased and my chest tightened. Everyone was waiting. The stares were penetrating, but I pushed the anxiety aside, cleared my throat, and began.

"My name is Chad Hepler. I was born in Boston, Massachusetts, and at the age of three my family moved to Alpharetta, Georgia. I grew up in a Christian-based family with both my Mom and Dad and a brother. My brother is older by three years.

"Throughout my childhood, my parents have always been very loving and supportive, and my brother has been my best friend. You could not ask for a better family situation. I began my schooling at a private Christian school, but changed schools to another private Christian school in the fourth grade. I am still currently attending the same school.

"I was always active throughout my life and participated in many sports, including soccer, baseball, and basketball. I grew up like an average kid, spending my summers either at the pool, selling lemonade, or playing video games. My friends and I also enjoyed playing whatever sport or game we could think of. Some of our favorites were soccer, baseball, roller hockey, 'gotcha,' football, and capture the flag.

"Religion was also a dominant activity. I grew up going to Sunday school, church, and other religious functions. Between private Christian schools and church functions, I developed a strong belief in Christianity.

"Throughout elementary school, I played on recreational basketball, soccer, and baseball leagues. Later, in junior high, I continued with my love for sports by competing on the seventh and eighth grade basketball teams and track team. Pole vaulting ended up being my main focus.

"The summer before ninth grade was my first encounter with alcohol, marijuana, and amphetamines. The boys I hung out with in my neighborhood attended the local public school and started experimenting with alcohol and drugs at a much earlier age than guys at my school. The first time I tried marijuana was at the age of thirteen. It was late one night and my friends and I were on the porch of a neighbor's house. The feeling the high gave me was the best thing that had ever happened. I loved it from the beginning. A few days later was my first encounter with alcohol. One night, my friends and I were camping out on the trampoline in my backyard when my buddies were talking about these little liquor bottles they had found. The bottles were collector-style bottles that were left behind by the previous owners of the house. Apparently, the boys had already drunk a few the night before and were discussing doing it again. It sounded like fun, so I asked if I could join. The night progressed and once it was late enough, we snuck in to the basement, gandering at all the different bottles. They were enticing, magical, and glowing with mystery. There must have been fifty. We each snatched three and took off. Without a chaser, I quickly downed all three back to back. The taste was brutally disgusting, but it didn't matter. The warming burning sensation was enjoyable. The burning seemed to tingle my throat and stomach. Only minutes later, the world tilted and before I knew it I was drunk. It was amazing. Instantly, the alcohol produced a completely different perspective of the world. I ran around drunk underneath the summer moonlight, having the time of my life.

"Weeks later my dad, mom, brother, and I had just finished eating dinner, but my mom had some unfortunate news to tell us. She reached out to my dad and grasped his hand, and I assumed the worse. Calmly but confidently, my mom announced she had been diagnosed with breast cancer. Instantly a sick feeling churned in my stomach. The C word. There is nothing worse. I was speechless and didn't know what to think as she explained that surgery was necessary to remove the breast. Fortunately, she would have it reconstructed from fat in her stomach. She also explained that she would have to undergo four rounds of chemotherapy, causing her hair to fall out.

"My dad's eyes began tearing up and his knuckles turned white as he gripped her hand tighter. The emotions were overwhelming. I had never seen my dad cry and it caused my tears to swell. It was terrible. We all cried. My mom was our rock, our support, our glue, and the thought of not having her was unbearable.

"That type of news is what every family prays not to hear and it threw me for a loop, but my faith in God was still strong and I knew without a doubt in my mind that he would not call her this early. Later that night, I told her that I had faith that she would be just fine and would get through this without any issue. She collapsed into my arms. I held her with all my love and she cried and cried and cried. I cried too.

"Despite the worst news of my life, my drive for impairment continued growing. Substances offered too many wonderful things, like confidence, fun, acceptance, and relaxation. The idea of causing my parents stress never crossed my mind. Whenever I could get my hands on weed from the local pot dealer or successfully steal booze from one of our parents' cabinets, I would party my head off.

"One afternoon, one of my friends learned that you could take Adderall to get messed up. Adderall was a different type of curiosity and I had no reserves about giving the drug a shot. The same neighbor who had the liquor bottles also had a prescription for Adderall. The pills were out in the open and free for our taking. We would pop anywhere from three to five of the ten milligram pills and be absolutely lit all day at school. The feeling Adderall gave me in a large amount was a feeling of complete euphoria and numbness. All I wanted to do was have a heart-to-heart with anyone I came in contact with. The feeling would last for about twelve hours then I would crash—depressed and lethargic all the day. Because the come-down was so intense, Adderall became only an occasional drug. For the most part, I stuck to smoking weed and getting drunk during tenth grade. Weed became my new best friend. It helped me feel comfortable around my peers and made school interesting. I would smoke several times a day, starting in the morning and ending before bed. Drinking wasn't nearly as enticing at the time, but I did like to get drunk on the weekends.

"Further into my junior year, two days before my seventeenth birthday, I was arrested for possession of marijuana. During this same time period, I started experiencing an unusual amount of anxiety and depression. A doctor prescribed an antidepressant/anxiety medication. The pills helped, but I continued with the illegal substances. The mixture of depression, anxiety, substances, and medication created a recipe for 'I don't give a damn.' Nothing mattered to me and I had no priorities, causing school to become an occasional occurrence. I mean, why go to school when everything felt too good? On the days I didn't skip, a few buddies and I would bail on chapel to go smoke at a nearby parking lot or inside a car on campus. Sometimes I drank before school or during chapel. My grades, of course, slipped, resulting in the lowest GPA I could have ever imagined, a 1.9 average. Not even high enough to graduate.

"My junior year was also the time I experienced my first love. Around the same time I started the medication, a girl and I started dating. It was halfway through my junior year and I fell head over heels for her. Since I never had a serious relationship, I knew this was it. She was the one and the relationship became like a drug. I even slowed down on drinking and using and came off the medication. We dated for eight months, but at the beginning of my senior year, we broke up. Alone, lost, and depressed, I became bitter. I had never experienced heartbreak and for me it was traumatic. Turning back to my best friends, substances, I started using to a new extreme. I drank at night to numb the pain. It didn't work. Actually, it made things worse, but I kept trying. I would stay up late into the night, using and drinking. Every day at school I was a zombie and all of my relationships suffered, especially with my parents. I kept as much distance between them and myself at all times. Some nights I was so messed up I would scream, yell, and curse for no real reason. There was so much frustration and anger, and punching holes in walls became a new hobby. I even started lying to my brother, the one person I knew wouldn't pass judgment, but still I lied.

"One night my brother and I went to Athens, Georgia, to visit a few friends. We drank so much downtown that I punched him in the face after a small argument. A cop almost arrested us, but instead he demanded we get in a cab and leave downtown. The next morning, I woke up with no memory of the incident. It wasn't until I saw his black, purple, yellowish swollen eye that I remembered. I felt terrible and a pile of remorse and shame came over me. Despite my many apologies, I still don't think he has forgiven me.

"I also became distant from my true friends at school. These friends actually cared about me and were always there in times of need, but they didn't use. I found myself hanging out with only people that used. It was uncomfortable to be around people that were sober.

"Apparently my parents think I have a problem, and two nights ago I was awakened by them and an escort service. I attempted to get away, but was unsuccessful. That is why I am here standing before you in the middle of nowhere on the other side of the country."

A round of applause echoed through the dining hall and I strolled back to my seat. As I sat down, I thought about how ironic it was that I was just rewarded with a cheerful round of applause for telling my tale of darkness. Well, maybe not my whole tale. I left out the parts of the harder drugs I used. *Maybe they will let me go home now. I hope.* The less I told, the better. It was imperative to make myself look as good as possible, but still tell enough that I looked like I wasn't lying. People who just smoke pot, drink, and do a few pills don't have a problem. There was still a glimmer of hope.

The meeting closed with the usual prayer and we were adjourned for the evening. Phone calls! I rushed to the trailer to get a good spot in line, knowing I had to call one of my friends. They had to know where I was, and as far as I knew, no one knew what happened—that I had been stolen from existence. Reaching into my pocket, I pulled out a calling card and dialed the numbers. The phone was ringing and excitement surged through me.

My friend answered, "Aah, hello?"

"Jamie!" I exclaimed, "It's Chad."

"Whooooaaaa... No way! Dude, where are you? I heard you got shipped off."

"Yeah, man, it's ridiculous. I got woken up in the middle of the night and hauled off. I'm in Montana."

"Whaaat, Montana! Are you kidding? Damn, that's nuts... Hey, I've got Mike here, too, hold on a sec." He put the phone on speaker and Mike joined in, "Chaddy B, is that you?"

I gave a little laugh, "Yeah, man, what's up?"

"Damn, dude, I talked to your brother yesterday and he told me everything. You all right?"

"I'm OK, but better now that I can talk to y'all. What's going on?"

"Nothing, just hanging out. But man, we have been planning on coming to break you out. I'll drive three days to get there, no problem."

"I wish. I can't believe I'm here, but I did learn from one of the guys that once you turn eighteen, they can't force you to stay here and you know that I turn eighteen tomorrow..."

"All right, we'll see you in a couple days."

I chuckled nervously, realizing they were kidding, but I started contemplating really trying to leave. We continued to talk about what was going on back home and all about where I was until the fifteen-minute time limit ran out. It was so annoying when the time ran out. This nerdy night tech would abruptly interrupt the conversation from a phone on the other side of the trailer. You would be in the middle of sentence like, "Yeah, wow that sounds like—" then his obnoxious voice would announce, "You've got thirty seconds, say your good byes and hang up." It filled me with anger every time, but there was nothing I could do except just say goodbye.

Leaving the trailer, I thought more about leaving. *Is it really possible? Can I do it? It seems like such a long shot, but it would be so great. I'd be gone! Screw this place.* Getting back to my bunk, I stared at the ceiling, running through all the factors. I started with the negative ones first. Let's see... Well, I would have to march a couple miles in the snow to get to the road. There I would have to hitchhike who-knows-how-many miles to get to the nearest city, then I would have to catch some sort of charter bus line across the country. I wouldn't have much to eat and would have no money and might have to sleep out in the cold.

The negative factors were a bit rough and started to seem unbearable, but the thought of getting out outweighed anything. Being on my own sounded so sweet. I could do whatever I wanted with no one bothering me, no one controlling me, just pure freedom. I could get messed up without any consequences, whenever I want, whatever I want. Life would be great. I had never experienced true freedom and here stood my chance.

After hopping down from the bunk, I crossed over to talk to Rob. He was lying on his bed reading a recovery book, which was the only reading material around. No interest to me, I'd rather stare at the wall than read about alcoholics. Sitting down on the far side of his bed, I began asking questions about escaping. He explained how he went through the same thing when he first got here and stashed a bunch of apples and bananas before trying to escape in the middle of the night.

Sitting up in bed he said, "Yeah, man, I had it all worked out. I was going to panhandle fifty bucks to buy a ticket for a Greyhound bus ticket. You know, for fifty bucks you can go anywhere."

"What! Fifty bucks for anywhere! No way."

"I swear, man, anywhere for fifty bucks."

Excitement surged through me. *I can do this. I can really leave. Hell yes, I'm getting out of here. Screw this garbage. Thank you, Rob. What a life saver.*

"Why didn't you leave?"

"Dude, I tried. The damn night tech, Willie, caught me walking though the fields. After that, I just figured I'd stay. Besides, I probably would have been screwed not having a place to stay or whatever."

Despite his failed attempt, the conversation gave me a sense of hope and the idea of leaving sounded perfect. *I'll figure it out. This is great!* I talked with him for a few more minutes before retiring for the night.

The next morning was Monday, the beginning of treatment week. Lame! In order to get to breakfast by seven, Carsten woke us at six thirty, which really pissed me off. It was still dark when I stepped out of the cabin. The morning air was frigid, piercing through my clothes as I slipped and slid all the way down the sidewalk. *What am I doing here? I need to leave.* Sitting by the morning fire, I tried to bring blood back to my fingers as I thought more about escaping.

After breakfast we participated in the reading from the daily recovery book and circled up again with our arms around one another's shoulders, reciting the closing serenity prayer. By now I knew the words and actually recited them, just to look good. "God grant us the serenity to accept the things we cannot change, the courage to change the things we can, and the wisdom to know the difference."

We were given thirty minutes to freshen up before starting the group sessions. Unsure of what to expect, I went in with the mindset that I would probably just observe and not really participate. I entered the room where there were seven guys sitting in a circle along with a counselor, Tim. It seemed so surreal. *Am I really in a support group? What the hell!*

With a big sigh, I took my seat and we began. Tim declared that today was Thomas's day to do Knees to Knees. He pulled out a sheet of paper with a series of questions and handed it to Chris. In the middle of the circle was a small circular chair with wheels but no back. Tim instructed, "All right, Thomas, take a seat and shimmy up to Chris to touch knees."

Chris cleared his throat and began reading the first question. The questions required Thomas to commit to sobriety and demand his respect to every other patient. The sheet was passed around the circle and one by one everyone went knees to knees with him. The sheet came to me, and I read through it like a robot. *This is stupid.*

The exercise seemed pointless until Thomas came knees to knees with the counselor. He started off slow and calm, until he started wiggling his words deep into Thomas's conscious, dancing on all the things he had done wrong—including the people he had hurt. The further Tim went, the more serious he became, and the more trouble Thomas had hiding his shame. It wasn't long before Thomas cracked and started bawling—just what the exercise was meant to do.

Thomas joined back in to the circle and was given a few tissues. Everyone talked about the exercise, while I remained quiet. *What on earth is going on?* Without anything to say, I started imagining myself going through the exercise. *I would never crack. I'm strong. Only losers crack. I'm made of iron.*

During lunch three boys came up to the area where I had given my life story and started stating random things. The first boy was clearly nervous, stumbling all over his words, "To-to-to-today I-I-I-I am thankful fo-fo-for my family, my hel-hel-health, and my friendships." Everyone gave a round of applause. The next boy spoke, "Today I am not going to dwell on my past and work on my sobriety." Another round of applause. A third boy spoke, "Today I am proud of myself, because I am working hard at my recovery." The boys returned to their seats and everyone went back to eating. *What was that?* Confused, I nudged Germ and whispered, "Dude, so, what was that all about?"

He was still chewing his sandwich, but managed to mumble, "Lunch libs."

"Huh?"

Before speaking, he swallowed his bite. "You'll have to do it, too. Everyone does. The counselors require you to state something at lunch like that for a couple weeks. I'm starting tomorrow. It's lame."

After lunch we were allowed an hour of free time before going back to the Treatment House for the next three hours. It felt like the day was never going to end. *I really need to leave! It's so cold.*

Entering the Treatment House, I found the boys standing around cutting up and conversing. Feeling lonely and out of place with none of my friends, I stood against the wall until one of the counselors walked in and instructed, "Get to work." *Work? I don't have work. This is so dumb. Get me out of here.*

Only seconds later, Carsten walked in and called me back to his office. He plopped down in his chair and instructed, "Take a seat." He switched on the desk lamp, and with his eyes closed, he began rubbing his forehead. "OK, Chad, you are going to..." he stopped, but with his eyes still closed, continued to rub his forehead. He looked deep in thought.

Like he just had some great epiphany, his hands came off his forehead and his eyes opened. "You are going to write a list of thirty negative things about drinking and using."

Not sounding hard I agreed, "All right, no problem."

I stood up and started to exit the room.

"Wait!"

Stopping in my tracks, I looked back. With his hands behind his head, and leaning back in his chair, he said, "Make that a hundred."

"Aah, OK." I left the room. *This is lame, but just play along and they'll realize you don't need to be here. Yeah, great idea. Just make the list.* In order to pry my brain for negatives, I starting playing out different memories of using drugs while I searched for a spot among the couches. The most vivid was the night I ate some sort of hallucinogen called GHB. I think.

Shortly after my first love and I broke up, two months into my senior year, I really went off the deep end. Drinking, smoking, and occasional drugging was my life. One night I received a phone call that an acquaintance of mine was selling an imitation version of LSD called GHB. It was a Tuesday night and I debated, knowing I had school in the morning. *School's important. Sorta. But a hallucinogen...Now that sounds fun.*

Substances were way more important, and for ten dollars I purchased two drops. The acquaintance dropped the clear tasteless drops on my tongue, but it was getting close to curfew. By this point my parents had me on a tight leash so, trying to avoid any conflict with them, I went home on time. Conflict gets in the way of using— that's the last thing I wanted.

The acquaintance and I planned to meet up in a few hours. Acquaintances were all I had. My real friends were gone. Only people who liked to use were my "friends." Besides, real friends don't let friends use drugs. *Yeah. Whatever. That's lame.*

An hour later, as I waited for my parents to click off their light, the drug started kicking in. Completely covered in glow-in-the-dark stars, the multi-level ceiling of my bedroom started morphing and twisting. The twirling stars on the fan blades created an image of planet rings floating back and forth among the galaxy. It was a tripper's dream, and my eyes were playing games. Staring at the ceiling, I giggled and smiled, watching the stars run like ants all over the ceiling and walls. The rings from the fan bounced from left to right, and trippy music tickled my ears. It was so cool. Everywhere I looked, the stars would follow, running, morphing, twisting. I laid on my bed, frozen in the dark. There was no need to move with this show. It was like my own personal laser show. What a trip.

Hours passed and it was getting late. Three in the morning had just ticked over and the red lights from the clock were bouncing up and down. My body was tired, my brain hurt. I was ready for the show to end. The drug wasn't. Closing my eyes, I tried to force myself to sleep, but every time I shut them, the world twisted and turned like the rings from the fan. Realizing sleep wasn't going to happen, I tried to call my acquaintance. Of course, no answer. He couldn't be sleeping, though, so I called and called and called. Nothing. No answer. And my brain began squirming. I at least wanted to talk to someone. Anything to get out of my own head.

Five in the morning ticked over. Desperate, I tried and tried to sleep, but my brain continued to squirm. There was nothing that could take the squirming away. The time came when I was supposed to be waking up for school. Cracked out but trying to piece my brain together, I stumbled to the shower for help. All thought processing was gone, and even forming a clear sentence felt like a battle.

The sun was up and I drove to school. The hallucinations were gone, but it felt like someone had taken a shotgun to my head. The idea of school sounded like a disaster, but still I pretended to convince myself I needed to go. On the way, I picked up a fellow using acquaintance. After I explained that I had been up all night tripping, he felt I shouldn't go to school. What a good friend. He knew what was best for me... It didn't take much to derail my half-hearted attempt at going to school. It's just that I felt guilty for skipping so much school already, but he had a better idea. Good thing he had ideas. I couldn't think two seconds ahead, but still I was the one driving. After a few phone calls, we drove over to a dealer's house. My acquaintance was into stimulants and was clearly seeking something.

Pulling into a small, two-story house, I could only imagine what we were getting. Well, maybe I couldn't imagine since imagination required too much thinking. I was just going with whatever. He seemed excited and said, "Come on, follow me. It's cool, I promise."

The house was plain but clean, and he instructed me to stay in the entranceway. I started to feel depressed as I watched him disappear down the stairs. Awkward and out of place, I stood quietly. The house was so quiet and so still, and I was starting to freak out. The anxiety was building and my emotions were all over the place. Too many emotions! Panic was stirring. *I should be at school... Why did I stay up all night? Life sucks. Who am I? What am I doing? You're fine, just chill out. He's getting something good, just stay calm. What do I do? Aaaaaah!*

Finally, he reappeared with a smile and relief washed over me. My brain came back to reality and I noticed the small baggie in his hand. Walking quickly through the house, we strolled onto the back porch and he poured a clear pile of powder across a glass surface.

"What's that?"

Staring at the pile, he pulled out a small razor blade and declared, "Meth."

Meth! What! Really? It was the dirtiest of all drugs in my mind. *Hmm, but I've never done it. Might as well try it.* After bringing a rolled up dollar bill to my nose, I leaned down and snorted. It burned and burned and burned, and my eyes watered. I had never felt such a burn. It hurt, but it passed and the high set in. The feeling was much like the Adderall, but I felt even more cracked out. I felt so dirty, so cracked out and so gross. We took turns, passing the bill back and forth until it was gone, but he wanted more. Quickly disappearing again, I watched him leave, debating if I would do any more. I looked around the woods, trying to make sense of my life. The drug had my brain racing. *What am I doing? Who am I? Is this what I've become? Doing drugs?* My mind pulled in different directions. I felt so dirty and desperately wanted the drugs to wear off. A glimmer of clarity shot through my soul and the thought of being sober sounded so much more appealing. *I should be in school. What am I doing? Get me out of here.* When he returned, I refused.

Fifteen minutes later, he finished and we actually went to school, but it was hell. Concentration was impossible, but at least I was there. I actually felt good about being at school. The second it ended, I raced home and slept through the night. Well, except for when my parents came in to see if I was alive. "I'm fine... just sick... need sleep."

The next morning I woke at the crack of dawn and realized it was time for school. I slid off the bed slowly and painfully. My stomach churned, my thoughts were broken, and my soul hurt. *Never again will I go through that.* The shower was the best I could do to shake the feeling of crud.

The memory of the drug experience was more than enough to start my list of One Hundred Negative Things About Using Alcohol and Drugs. Finding an empty spot on the worn, musty couch, I plopped down and began writing.

<u>One Hundred Negative Things About Using Alcohol and Drugs</u>

- Anxiety
- Sleeplessness
- Hurt Relationship with Dad
- Hurt Relationship with Mom
- Money
- Jail
- Arrested
- Fines
- Probation
- Loss of friends
- Poor school performance
- Less physical activity
- Poor diet
- Poor workouts
- Poor track practice
- Skipping school
- Skipping track practice
- Headache
- Irritability
- Depression
- Hangover
- Loss of concentration
- Bad attitude
- Loss of religious views
- Damaged liver
- Damaged lungs
- Damaged muscles
- Loss of other hobbies
- Drinking and driving
- Smoking and driving
- Not solving problems
- Not preventing problems
- Yelling
- Cursing
- Screaming
- Mandatory community service
- Paranoia
- Fear
- Not caring
- Not loving
- False friendships
- No emotional growth
- Loss of girlfriend
- Alcohol dependency
- Drug dependency
- Alcohol poisoning
- Hurt relationship with brother
- Rehabs

- Money spent on rehabs
- Time wasted
- Distant
- Consumed lifestyle
- Unmet goals
- Not pursing rewarding things
- Coasting through life
- Not succeeding
- Stomach problems
- Throwing up
- Embarrassment
- Regrets
- MIPs
- Criminal record
- Doing things you wouldn't normally do
- Loss of control
- Mental addiction
- Brain alterations
- Doing stupid things
- Doing wrong things
- Susceptibility to illness
- Self-absorbed
- "Whiney"
- Labeled a certain way
- Loss of self-respect
- Loss of respect from friends
- Loss of respect from family
- Hazy feeling
- False sense of reality
- False sense of confidence
- Unable to sharpen social skills
- Only comfortable if drunk or use
- Inability to truly know myself
- Not dealing with stress the right way
- Losing keys
- Losing phone
- Breaking phone
- Damages to car
- Unable to save money
- Getting into fights
- Saying things I didn't mean
- Punching holes in walls
- High blood pressure
- Dehydration
- Tolerance
- High risk choices
- DUI school
- Lawyer fees
- Blackouts
- Brain damage
- Quitting jobs
- Cancer

The list was too easy to create, and for the first time in my life I looked at the negative side of using drugs and alcohol. Being able to so quickly make a list of one hundred negative consequences sparked a new side of thinking. I felt ashamed for the first time. I quickly folded the sheet and stuck it in a manila folder just to get it out of sight. But this new side of thinking wasn't letting me shake the list. *Maybe I do need to be here. Maybe I was out of control. I don't know. I don't have a problem though. But the list. Whatever. Not me. I was just having fun.*

Snuffing out the glimmer of clarity, my addictive side regained control. It's not like creating a list was going to change my life, but for the first time a rational thought made it to my conscious thinking. Steps were beginning in the right direction. Small, small, small baby steps, but steps nonetheless. Picking apart an addiction is more complicated than life itself, but you have to start somewhere. You can't eat an elephant in one bite. Right?

After dinner, the cook came walking out with a homemade birthday cake. I had almost forgotten today was my birthday. It warmed my soul to see her blue eyes sparkling behind her glasses.

She exclaimed, "Happy birthday! Now make a wish and blow them out."

Wishing I could escape from the rehab facility, I took in a deep breath and blew out all 18 candles. A small, half-hearted round of applause echoed through the dining hall. Germ patted me on the back. Ironically, a warm, happy feeling enveloped me. Birthdays were always my favorite, but I just wished I were hanging out with friends smoking and drinking, not sitting at rehab.

I was officially eighteen, officially an adult and officially able to leave the facility. No one could stop me. What a powerful feeling. *No one can tell me to do anything. I'll show them...I'm getting out of here.* Leaving sounded so sweet, but the journey sounded so terrible. No money. No shelter. No transportation. And freezing weather. Could I really make it?

Glancing out the window, I noticed the snow was coming down hard and my mind began leaning toward staying. The blazing fireplace only reinforced the thought. *Wait. No. Just go. I can be on my own and get messed up. It'll be perfect. But how do I get there? I can't make it. Too far. Too cold. But freedom. No rules. No, I can't. What do I do?* My addictive side and sober side battled for minutes.

The kitchen caught my attention. I won't have food. I must have food. Going more than four hours without food was bad enough, let alone days.

That was it. The clincher. Food pushed me off the fence. My sober side was winning and desperately tried to convince the addictive side. *Come on. Realistically, the Dub is not that bad. Think about it... True... But freedom. Yeah, but with what price? The price is not even attainable.*

SLAM! The cook dropped a Styrofoam bowl of chocolate cake and vanilla ice cream right in front of me. Perfect timing. The thought of leaving was extinguished. I was staying.

For the next couple days I began assimilating to the center, the guys, and the treatment sessions. Every day we spent three hours in group therapy in the morning and three more in the afternoon. Every night, there was a recovery meeting and everything was, of course, mandatory. Thursday came around and I was informed I was going through the Knees to Knees exercise. I was nervous, but convinced I would be fine, I prepped myself for the counselor's verbal attacks. I was stronger than Thomas. I'd be fine. He's going to say whatever he can to break me—it won't work.

We entered the Treatment House and one of the boys wheeled the swivel chair over. Confidently, I plopped down and rolled around the circle answering the usual questions as I pledged my commitment to each boy and the program. Finishing with the guys, I shimmied my way over to the counselor, touched knees, and stared back into his glare.

My expression was calm and confident, but he just kept staring at me.

Silence...

Clearly stalling, he rubbed his beard a few times. *Speak already. Come on. Let's get this over with. You're not going to win.* Finally he opened his mouth, "Well, Chad, clearly you know why you are here."

I nodded my head, and he paused, just staring. *Do I know? I pretended, but I don't need this. Doesn't matter, just play along.*

Breaking the silence, the tone of his voice became more serious, "You nod your head in agreement, but I don't believe you have bought in to this program." Confused, I immediately attempted to rebut, but he sternly interrupted, "Don't speak yet, just listen."

Pause...

I couldn't figure out if the pause was for effect or if he was trying to read me or what he was doing, but it was awkward and it started to make me feel uncomfortable. Shifting my weight from side to side, repositioning the way I was sitting, I tried to get away from the glare. It was piercing and uncomfortable and the silence heightened the anxiety. *Must remain strong. No weakness.*

He opened his mouth, "You are not being honest with everyone in this program." Lifting his right hand, he pointed around the room, "I mean, you went around the room telling these guys that you would do whatever it would take to make this program work and to commit to recovery, but I think that's a load of crap."

Pause...

Quit staring at me... What are you doing?

Pause...

"That is what you do best... lie... isn't it?"

What! Who is this guy? That's stupid... My eyebrows lowered, expressing my disbelief as my confusion grew, but I remained silent. He continued, "I mean, you've been lying to your parents for years and it definitely doesn't stop there. You lie to your brother, to your friends, hell, you even lie to yourself."

Pause...

I tried to make sense of where he was going. It was so irritating.

"Just recently you lied about your drug usage on the substance abuse evaluation."

What! How!? How did he know that? A strange nervous feeling of complete shock pulsed through my body. The only thing I could do was look around the room, trying to avoid eye contact with him. His glare was too strong, though, and I was exposed. Ashamed of the drugs I had done, I desperately yearned for no one to know, but he knew. How? How? How? My mind raced to piece it together, but nothing made sense. Unable to dwell long, he pulled my attention back with another set of painful accusations.

"You lie, you steal, you wreck people's cars, you go off-roading on people's lawns, you skip school, you yell and curse at your parents," he abruptly paused and stared at me in disgust.

Hearing all my negative actions lumped up in one sentence put everything in a new perspective. Immediately, the shame hit me like a ton of bricks and I wanted to hide. But my ego stood strong. *Can't be broken, can't be broken, can't be broken. You knew this was coming. Think about something else. Anything but his words.*

Beaches, puppies, bed, whatever... anything. I tried to push his words out of my head, but they were building.

"You punch holes in walls, you cause everyone stress by your actions, you can't be trusted with anything, you say mean things to your ex-girlfriend. I mean, tell me where to stop. The list goes on and on. What a piece of garbage you are."

Everything he said was true and there was nothing I could do to make it untrue. The guilt kept building. The shame was peaking. *No, push it away. Don't listen. Don't let him break you.* I tried. It worked a little bit, but he glared and glared and glared.

His voice was still stern, "What is it going to take for you to change?"

Pausing even longer, my mind raced. I felt the need to answer, but nothing came to mind. My nerves were exploding, but on the outside I kept my cool. I hoped.

Finally he broke the eerie silence. His tone shifted to quiet and calm, "You can't go on living like this. It's not right, it's not fair to the ones who love you. You're not just hurting yourself, you're hurting everyone around you: your parents, your brother, your extended family, your friends."

He paused again to let the words sink in. The drastic change of tones played with my emotions and I tried to shake the words, but there were too many. It felt like the Persian army shooting a million fiery arrows, and no matter how hard I tried I couldn't block them all. I was doing my best to stay strong, but my cool image was slipping. The words were too strong. They cut deep. *Don't break. Don't break. You can't let him win.* He was winning. He was breaking me. He knew it. I was slipping and there was nothing I could do about it.

His voice went to a mere whisper, full of concern, "Chad, your life is on the line here. You have used up every second chance and I'm afraid that this is your last one. Your family can't take it anymore. They have had enough, and if you don't let this program help you, then you will be on your own for the rest of your life, or even worse, you'll be dead. You have been given more chances than you deserve and this is the final straw." He stared deep into my eyes, and I knew he could sense my guilt and shame. I looked down at the ground trying and trying to block him out, but it felt like his fingers were poking my heart.

Seconds passed before his next statement grabbed my attention, "Your Jeep is gone. Your parents are in the process of selling it to help pay for your second chance." My eyes shot straight up. A numb feeling echoed through my body. I had to speak, "What, what are you talking about?"

"Your parents are selling your Jeep, man."

I muttered, "You're kidding."

"Nope, it's gone, that's it. I mean, your parents warned you a million times about what would happen if you drank and drove, but you obviously couldn't have cared less."

He paused and stared at me.

No! Not my Jeep! My baby. No way!

"This really shouldn't be much of a surprise to you."

It was a surprise. I couldn't believe it. The phrase echoed through my head, *your Jeep is gone, your Jeep is gone,* but I quickly went into a state of denial. *He's lying. Surely not. No way.* Hopelessly looking up, I expected him to retract his statement. He said nothing. Just kept staring. His stare was all I needed to confirm that he wasn't lying, and just like that it was over. The final blow. The kill shot. Game over, and he knew it. My mouth quivered and my eyes swelled. I couldn't hold it back any longer and a small tear dropped from each eyelid and slid down my checks. No one spoke, no one moved. Nothing more needed to be said. He had done it. He had won. He had achieved his goal and all I could do was look down with my head hanging in utter defeat.

Phase One

I joined the group, wiped my eyes, and they began debriefing. Feeling embarrassed and broken, I remained quiet. I was just exposed and my wall of defense was gone. Behind the crumbled wall I stood weak, scared, and worried. There was no hiding. Every different piece of the wall, especially my stubbornness, was demolished. Stubbornness was the main ingredient for the wall. It kept all attempts of help far, far, far away. With stubbornness tossed aside, I soaked in the outside opinion. *Maybe they are right. I mean, my actions sounded so bad. I don't know.*

Is there a problem lying beneath? Maybe. Having my list of shame thrown in my face created a whole new perspective. It was new, weird, and different. No one ever called me out like that. Or maybe I was never sober enough to listen. But here, I had to listen. I couldn't escape. They forced my shame upon me, and it hurt. No drugs or alcohol to run to. Is this real life? I don't know, but it hurts. It hurts bad.

My mind had been in such a haze for the last three years, my decisions were never based on logic. They were more of an impulsive emotional reaction, especially decisions to use substances. Did the substances help or hurt? What came first, the chicken or the egg? In my mind they helped, or maybe I was just too foggy to realize they hurt. Did they create the problem, or was the problem already there?

The Knees to Knees exercise combined with the time away from drugs and alcohol were clearing my mind, though. It felt like a cloud was rising from my head and it felt great. I felt alive, and I was beginning to feel high on life for the first time in a long time. The exercise broke me, making me think in reality and it hurt, but moments later I felt refreshed—like I had taken a moral shower.

Seeing my skeletons through a clear set of eyes instead of behind the false screen of haze was inspiring. In the past, the constant nagging of guilt pushed me to keep using. Coming down from the fog meant facing the waiting list of amends and that was unbearable, too much for a sober mind. I had been hiding in the shadows, avoiding accountability for my actions, creating a plaque. The plaque stuck heavy on my mind and all over my soul. It was always there and always nagging, and there was no escaping it except through a substance. But the plaque was created from the substance. Treating a problem by using the problem as the solution? That doesn't make sense. Where did I go wrong?

Only through forced sobriety and heart-wrenching exercises would I begin to think I had the courage to move on. Realizing I might be able to do something about my actions helped boost my morale.

The rest of the day went much easier and the afternoon group focused on other issues besides me. What a relief. I couldn't handle any more intense therapy that day. When the treatment day ended, I could only hope I would receive a letter.

With his usual grim look, Willie came limping into the dining hall and started calling out names. Holding my breath, I waited. *Please. Please, someone send me a letter. I need to hear an outside voice! I need it! I need encouragement.*

Willie's scruffy voice announced, "Chad Hepler." *Yes!!* Jumping up like a contestant on the "Price Is Right," I ran toward him. As I reached him, he pulled out his pocket knife and slit open the envelope. He did a thorough search, and from his seat, handed the two letters to me, never making eye contact. Not even Willie's attitude could affect my mood, though. The letters were all we had, and pure joy flooded my emotions.

Before I opened them, I found a secluded spot at one of the picnic benches, sat down, and read the return addresses. The first one was from my brother and the second was from one of my high school female friends. Opening the letters, I could not hold back a smile. My brother wrote:

Chad,

Man, where do I start this letter? These last days since you have been gone have been, to say the least, very different. I came home after some of the most intense and stressful days to Mom and Dad and a very sleepy dog. There is no brother to laugh and joke with, or kick back and play Tiger Woods with. I'm definitely lonely around here. I miss you and want you to know how much you mean to me. Life just isn't the same around here; I can only imagine this is how you must have felt when I left for college. I am praying for you daily and want you to know I care about you tremendously. I hope God's blessings are raining on you while you're out there. Anyways, enough with all the mushy stuff, I'm just going to tell you what I have been up to around here.

I continued reading the next couple pages as he talked about all the fun things he had been doing and then he went into the closing of the letter

Chad, I cannot express to you how much you mean to me and how much I value our friendship. You have been my best friend since the day you were born and you will always be. I want my old brother back, the one who wasn't afraid to tell me the truth and helped me get through so many of my hard times. I really couldn't have done it without you. Keep your head on straight out there, let the fog clear out, and look at who and what's important to you, and know that there is no limit to how much your family loves you. Dad would have given everything including the clothes off his back to help you, Chad. They love you very much and so do I. Peace out homie homie, and I will see you shortly.

    Love,
    Matt

P.S. The beef-monster wants me to tell you she loves you and misses you.

I set the letter down and let out a small sigh. It was great to hear from my brother and comforting to know he wasn't angry or thinking anything bad. He was my support and I could always go to him with any problems, issues, or just when I needed advice. Nine times out of ten, he had already been through a certain issue that I was going through and would have the type of advice I needed to hear, not just what I wanted. The letter he had written only reinforced these feelings. I sat there in a moment of pure bliss as I thought about the good times we spent together.

I didn't dwell too long though. The next letter was waiting. On multi-colored paper with pink writing was a letter from my friend Lindsay. Unfolding the letter, a feeling of excitement raced through me. The bubbly writing said:

Chadday...What's up baby doll? How are you my love? I was so excited when your brother called to give me your address! I hate to hear about all of this but it might be for the better. I hope they aren't working you too hard. Anyways... we just got back from the class trip. (You didn't miss too much.)

OK...I really just want you to know that I love you so much and for the past week I have picked up the phone to call you and then I would remember you weren't here. Just think of this as a vacation. Just do what you're supposed to do so you can find the real Chad again. You mean so much to me and I want you to know I will never judge you in any way and that I am here if you ever need <u>ANYTHING.</u> You have always been the big brother I never had and I thank you for that. You always make me laugh and if I ever needed anything you were there for me. I miss you more than you will ever know. We are bored without you! Have as much fun as you can. Get buff and find the real you!! I am thinking and praying for you! You better write me back ASAP. I want to hear from you!!

Love Always,
Lindsay

P.S. Sorry I got a little sappy, but I mean every word of it.

To hear from one my high school friends meant the world to me and the joy and comfort I received from reading the letter was amazing. I was so worried that everyone was going to think I was a loser for being in rehab, but her letter shook those thoughts. I continued to sit on the picnic bench with my feet propped up, enjoying the feeling. It was so nice to hear the support and love expressed from the people I cared about.

Once the boys had finished cleaning the dining hall, we were dismissed for the evening until the nine o'clock p.m. recovery meeting. Instead of going to the cabin or the game shed, I sat out on the porch to reflect on the day. The sky was too beautiful not to. The setting sun painted a golden sky mixed with fiery reds and bright oranges. Beaming on the mountains were broken rays of the sun bouncing off the scattered pines, creating a million silhouettes. Puffy clouds glowed with strips of red, yellow, and orange and layers of light blues, medium blues, dark blues filled the horizon. The two mountains closest to the valley reflected the colors, casting their shadows down on the snow-covered fields. It was one of the most beautiful scenes I had ever witnessed and only at this moment could I truly appreciate it. The scene felt like my soul: warm, calm, and serene. I marveled at the beauty and the feeling of peace.

The next day was Friday, work day, and I spent the day with a counselor in the horse pastures, digging tracks to allow the metal gates to open. The snow had built up so much that the gates couldn't move an inch. We took turns since we only had one pick axe. One guy would shovel away the top layer of the fresh powder while the other thrust the axe into the three-inch layer of ice covering the ground. The small tip on the pick axe barely made an impact and after every thrust, only a small piece of the ice layer would chip away. The length of the track arched out about twenty feet long, and at this rate it seemed like we were going to be there for days. Needless to say, the project took almost the entire workday. I felt like I was turning into a snowman with the constant snow collecting on my shoulders and head. The cold air was brutal, and no matter how hard we worked, the zero degree weather was simply piercing.

Hours passed before we finished clearing the tracks. I prayed we be done even though there was about forty-five minutes left. To my disbelief, we were ordered to shovel trails from one building to another. It seemed like busy work to me. I hate busy work, but when the day finally ended, I was proud of myself for sticking with it. Not something I would normally do.

Later that evening I received more mail. The letters coming from family and friends were now pouring in. What a support system I had! It was comforting and encouraging. After watching a movie, we had free time so I lifted weights. I was definitely falling into the routine and beginning to be content with where I was. Acceptance was crucial. There was no other choice.

Saturday was another work day, and Sunday was a rest day with a recreational activity. We slept until ten a.m. and feasted on blueberry pancakes. For the recreational activity, Wilder Andy with his goofy grin took us on a hike up one of the smaller mountains. It was no easy task since our feet sank at least a foot with every step, but reaching the top of the mountain offered the reward. It was a sight of serenity. Much taller mountains engulfed us in all directions and the tall, powerful pines frosted with snow created an image of beauty below. In the valley was the facility, barely visible with only small dots of brown representing the buildings.

The next morning we woke up bright and early with the sun still asleep. It was Monday...treatment day. We all dreaded getting up. After breakfast, we went through the twenty minute reflection from the daily recovery book and then we were back for the three-hour group session.

Toward the end of the session, Carsten called me into his office and I followed him, actually feeling calm and comfortable. It was weird. He sat down and said, "So I wanted to see how you were doing."

"Pretty good," I responded.

He nodded, leaned back in the leather chair, looked around the room and then asked, "So how are you feeling?"

"Really good, actually. I feel like the fog has lifted off my head and I can think much clearly. Honestly, it's kind of weird feeling. I mean, I had forgotten what it was like to feel like this."

After years of impairment, sobriety did feel good. The daily high of drugs and alcohol eventually loses its strength and simply becomes normal feeling. A mental tolerance had been built for years in my head, so my brain had become used to the high. Being forced to come out of the cycle felt like a high itself. To me, high is any feeling other than "normal." Drugs and alcohol had felt normal for so long that all of a sudden, being clean didn't feel normal. It felt like a high, but without the baggage of shame, lies, and guilt. It felt great.

Breaking the cycle of the "normal" feeling is the hardest part since life becomes a constant cloud. Even if you aren't actually high, the haze and cloudy feeling is more than enough to keep you out of reality. That is the reason why it is almost impossible to convince someone to change unless they have been clean for enough time to erase the haze. Even if an individual wants to get sober, the drugs floating around in the system will speak louder than any good intention. Without being forced into the rehab, I would have never entered on my own. Not a chance. No way. But for the first time in a long time, I felt clean. Not necessarily sober, but clean. Being clean had to come first, though. It's a prerequisite. Sober is different from clean in that sober is a state of mind, whereas clean or not clean simply refers to whether or not there is a chemical in your body. Sobriety requires a new way of thinking. A way of thinking that yearns to live a life without chemicals and the desire to do whatever it takes to avoid using the chemicals. At this moment I was clean, but not sober. However, clean felt like a high and it was beginning to convince me to follow the sober path.

Carsten respond, "Well, good. I'm glad. That's good to hear. It is definitely different, isn't it?" He cracked a smile, and I nodded my head in agreement. Leaning down from the chair, he disappeared behind the desk, but I could hear him sliding open a drawer and shuffling through the files. He eventually reappeared holding several pieces of paper stapled together. Dropping the packets on the desk, he slid it toward me and said, "This is your Phase One packet. You will need to fill out by answering the questions with complete honesty and then present it to the group during the sessions."

I picked up the sheet, took a quick glance, and replied, "No problem."

He looked back, his expression turned serious. "All right, Chad, we need to talk about a few things."

Oh no. That sounds bad... Nervousness filled my chest, but curiosity filled my mind.

He continued, "Family Week is coming up next week and you need to get honest."

What! Family Week! I had no idea there was a Family Week. It sounded terrible, but I had to know more. "Aah, what exactly is Family Week?"

He leaned farther back in the leather chair and used a calming tone. "Well, starting Monday of next week, your parents and your brother will be here. They will be participating in treatment with you for the entire treatment week."

Instantly, a million different thoughts filled with fear, anxiety and nervousness swirled through my brain. My eyes darted around the room. Thinking. Thinking. Thinking. The looks of horror streaked across my parents' faces haunted every thought. There were so many things they didn't know. My drug history, the wreck in the neighborhood, skipping school, the list goes on. I couldn't even begin to imagine telling them.

Carsten must have sensed my fear. He interrupted my panicked thoughts.

"You'll be all right. All you need to do is be honest."

Honest! My life has been one giant lie. I can't be honest! So many things had been hidden, but I could sense he knew I was hiding things. But how much did he know? Deciding to probe his mind, I asked, "So, what do you mean by getting honest? I have been honest."

Leaning forward, getting close to my face he demanded, "Lay it all out. Tell all." He paused, letting my addictive side squirm. *No way. I can't do that. What do I say?* I said nothing and eerie moments passed before he continued.

"A good place to start is with your drug history." He looked at me like he was expecting an answer. Quickly darting my gaze up to the corner of the room, I debated. *I can't. Not a chance. Too much. Maybe a little bit. Just a few admissions. Wait. No. What do I do?*

His stare was upon me and I looked down at his face. His expression was practically pulling an answer out of me. *He must know, he has to know, he wouldn't keep probing if he didn't. What to do, what to do?* I continued to debate, but it didn't last long. I couldn't take it any longer and my conscious side took over. I looked down at the floor, shuffled my feet, let out a sigh, and finally admitted, "OK, OK, so I lied about my drug use." I looked back up at him, expecting a response. He said nothing, just looked back at me. *He wants more. Great. Do I really have to tell the details? Well, it's too late now not to.*

"I've done cocaine, meth, Ecstasy, mushrooms, GHB, a variety of pills, Adderall, weed, and alcohol."

I gazed past him in a blank stare. *Did I really just say that? Wow!* I had finally admitted my history to someone and I was still alive. Unsure of his reaction, my nervousness hid my relief. He leaned back in his chair, nodded his head a few a times and responded, "All right, good. That's a good start."

A start? That's it? A start? It felt like I just conquered a mountain and he called it a start. I wasn't sure what I expected him to say, but I thought it would be more than that. Maybe a high five or "Great job" or "Well done." Nope. Just "a start."

"Now," he looked around the room, "what else do you need to get honest about?"

His gaze fell back to me. He was giving me that same look that felt like his fingers were shifting through my brain like a filing cabinet. *They know everything, but how? I don't get it.* I started to panic again. I debated, thinking about what to say. Deciding to go with the easy route, I responded, "Nothing, that's it."

The easy route was my favorite route. Just lie and I won't have to do anything. Lying kept me using and using kept me lying. If I lied, I didn't have to change. No, I'm not high. No, I'm not drunk. No, I went to school. Lie. Lie. Lie.

A moment of clarity created a dissonance about the lie, though. I thought about how good it felt to admit to my drug history and deep down I wanted to tell more, but I wasn't used to the awkward feelings of change. It did feel good to speak the truth, but conquering one mountain was enough. Lying was still easier, and he knew I was lying, but it didn't matter. Sure, his face held disappointment, but I just wasn't ready to tell any more. Realizing I had to say something I said, "Well, how about I just wait until Family Week and let it all go then."

I helplessly sat there waiting for him to approve. A few long moments passed before he responded, "OK, that's fine." He looked down at his watch and said, "Well, it's about lunch time. Today at lunch I want you to say three things you are thankful for." I agreed and we walked over to the dining hall.

At lunch, once I had finished my sliced peaches and turkey sandwich, I strolled up to the front of the picnic benches and faced the group of counselors, patients, and other staff members. I waited until the cloud of chattering quieted. Carsten, sitting right below me, finished chewing his last bite, looked up and asked, "Well, Chad, what have you got for us?"

Clearing my throat, I gazed past everyone and declared, "Today I am thankful for my family, my health, and this food." I heard a few agreements and I walked away. *That was way easier than I thought.*

During the three-hour afternoon session, my mind wandered to Carsten's speech about honesty. It made me cringe just thinking about my drug history and the thought of explaining it to my parents. Hard drugs were never discussed in the household. The regular occurrence of weed and alcohol was no problem, but hard drugs... no way. Maybe if they had seen me with them it might be different, but as far as I knew they had no idea. It wasn't like alcohol or weed, where I got caught red-handed. Like the time I was "studying" in my room, but really rolling a joint.

I was sitting at my desk, carefully breaking up a bag of marijuana with the rest of the bag sitting on my desk. My bedroom door sticks when it's closed, so I felt no need to lock it. It takes an effort to get the door open, which would give me plenty of time to hide the stash. Or so I thought. All of a sudden, the door popped. Someone was coming. Scurrying, I tried to cover everything with the scattered pieces of school notes. Before the door was fully open, everything was covered and I was good. I hoped. Numb with fear, I sat motionless at the desk as my mom came strolling in. She knew something was up and my face gave it away. Her hand reached to the papers. I had to stop her. "MOM! WHAT ARE YOU DOING? STOP!" She didn't even respond and grabbed the papers. It was over. The papers seemed to float away and there lay the bag of weed. Damn it. We were just getting to the point where they were trusting me again. It had been five months since the last time I was caught. This was the second time, at sixteen years old.

The first time was a month before I turned sixteen. I was going to be driving in less than a month and a half. During dinner I could sense something was wrong. I had never been caught before and they definitely didn't know anything. But something felt off. The usual happy mood seemed so stale. I tried to lighten the mood, but it went nowhere, so I became more anxious. As they cleared the table, their behavior and tone of voice signaled a "talk" was definitely coming. A few days earlier I had just spent all of the three thousand dollars I had saved for years on accessories for my Jeep. It was my baby, my life, but my dad owned the vehicle. He had bought it for me, so it was still his.

He pulled out the keys and dropped them on the table. Panic gripped me. *Not the keys, anything but those!* Anxiety clouded my thoughts and my vision. My sight felt like images on a roll of film instead of a continuous flowing picture. Reaching down by his side, he pulled up a small white box and plopped it on the table. My heart wrenched. *A HAIR TEST! WHAT! NO WAY!* On the front was a happy family smiling and gazing at each other. At the bottom was a bright orange sticker that read "Now Tests for Ecstasy." *This is bad. Really bad.* My dad's voice was stern and clear as he spoke.

"Chad, we know you have been drinking and doing drugs."

What! Did he really just say that! It was my worst fear. *What do I do? Just deny it.* I tried to speak, but he was having none of it.

"No need to lie, Chad. We know what you have been doing and, therefore, your mother and I have a decided to give you an option. If you admit to using drugs and alcohol, then you will be far better off. Now, would you like to tell us the truth?"

Far better off? What does that mean? His stare was reaching into my brain, searching for an answer. I wanted to admit it, but it just seemed too hard. *I can't. Maybe I should. He has to know.* The only problem was that I felt like admitting would be worse. *But that hair test. What on earth?* It was staring at me, filling me with anger, doubt, fear, and the unknown. I had to know what my options were.

Looking down at my feet, I mumbled, "What are the keys for?"

His voice stayed stern but calm. "Well, Chad, here is how this is going to work." My chest tightened. "You can either tell us you have been using, which I highly recommend, or you can deny and take this test." He flipped his hand over motioning to the box. "If you fail the test, your Jeep will be gone. Sold." He reached out for the keys, covering them under his palm. My heart sank. "However, if you admit, then you will have to wait an extra month before you can get your license, but your Jeep will be spared."

No way. I can't believe this. It felt like I was on a game show from hell. My dad was the announcer dressed in a devil costume with blazing puffs of fire lighting behind him. It felt like he was laughing as he told me my options. Hahahaha! Behind door number one you can risk everything and take this test, or you can jump off this never-ending cliff. The choice is yours. Hahaha.

I had been practically waiting all my life to start driving and now I had to wait another month. A month! It felt like years. *What will my friends think?* Clearly, I had to admit to it, though. My hair was so full of THC you could probably smoke it. With my eyes back on the floor I muttered, "I've gotten drunk and smoked marijuana, but only twice." It was a lie, but maybe it will help.

My mom's blue eyes, clouded with anger, were staring at me. She spoke, "I don't believe that."

"I promise, only twice, I didn't even like it." *Please buy the lie... please buy the lie.*

Silence. *What were they thinking?* Moments passed, then my dad spoke. "Chad, we know of more than two instances. Quit lying and tell us the truth."

How do they know everything? I don't get it. What is going on? I have to tell the truth. Without ever making eye contact, I admitted. "OK, OK, I've been smoking off and on for a year or so." That was the last thing I wanted to say. *Now they are going to be on to me forever. At least I still have my Jeep. Thirty days. Thirty days. Forever.*

It took a few months of demonstrating good behavior before they came off my case. Well, sort of. Micromanaging had become their new hobby and trust is only earned in our house. But a couple of months later, I decided to smoke in the bathroom. Wanting to be high all the time, I had to get clever when I couldn't escape from the parents. My shower area had one door that opened up to the two sinks, the shower, and the toilet area. There is another door by the toilet. Basically, there were two doors you can lock when using the commode. I turned on the shower to cover the noise, locked the first door, put a towel under the bottom crack and then locked myself in the toilet area. Turning on the bathroom fan, I thought for sure I was good to go. *Finally some peace!* I packed the bowl. The lighter sparked and I took a couple hits, exhaling the smoke up into the fart fan. Going for my third hit, I held the bowl to my mouth.

POW! The door flew open. Beyond stunned, I stood dazed like a deer in headlights. There stood my dad, his face glowing with anger. He didn't yell, though, just used a tone of voice that made me cringe. "What do you know, sucking on the pipe again? Real good. Real good, Chad." He yelled back over his shoulder. "HOLLIE, HOLLIE, you better come see this."

Stomp-stomp-stomp. Stomp. Her steps made my nerves twitch. She must have sensed something was up, based on her fast pace. Her head poked around the door frame with a shocked expression. "Oh, my God, no, no, not this again. No, please, oh no." She couldn't stand the sight. I was still standing there holding the bowl in my left hand and the lighter in my right, enveloped in a cloud of smoke. She ran away.

That night, the wall between my parents and me reached a new height. I was so tired of them trying to catch me and stop me from getting high. I just wanted to smoke and drink. *Why do you care you so much? Leave me alone.* It was an all-out battle. The more I got caught, the less I cared, but they tried everything to make me stop. They tried taking my car away, driving me to school, forcing me to talk to recovering addicts and alcoholics. Everything. But I just wanted to get high.

Never being caught red-handed with other drugs was what made me so nervous about getting honest. In my mind, smoking and drinking was nothing, but to admit to using hard drugs was a whole new concept. By admitting to the laundry list of drugs, I knew my parents would really think I had a problem. Weed and alcohol were nothing. Everyone does that. But Ecstasy, meth, cocaine, Adderall, pills, mushrooms...Well, it just sounds so bad. I at least liked to think I was not like that. Besides, image was everything. If I could just make myself look normal, then I could keep using. Lies. Lies. Lies. Anything to keep using.

The afternoon session dragged on and on, and I continued to squirm in thoughts of fear. Not knowing how they would react was the worst part. Either way, it couldn't be good. When the afternoon session did finally end, it felt like I was coming out of battle, a mental battle. My constant thoughts of worry had worn me out. It was never an easy day in rehab, and night time began to feel like a vacation. Simply not being in the session was such a relief that it did not matter what I was doing, just as long as I was not in the treatment sessions. Nights were spent writing letters, lifting weights, playing checkers, or just sitting on the porch breathing in the crisp mountain air. One thing was for sure, the cold air mixed with the freshness of the mountain pines was enough to clear anyone's head. The large snowflakes helped soothe my nerves as I watched them float back and forth until they joined their fellows in the snow.

The next day, the afternoon group session was held in the trailer where we made phone calls. It seemed weird, but I was too focused on wanting to present my Phase One packet. I sat in the circle, holding the packet, and announced, "I'm ready to present." Counselor Tim agreed and said if time permitted, we would get to it. *If time permitted? What? No. I want to present today no matter what. The faster I get through all this, the faster I go home. What the hell!* Pissed off but knowing I couldn't reveal my emotions, I remained quiet. Challenging the counselors never got anyone anywhere.

A few moments later, my least favorite counselor came walking in. He passed through the wooden doorframe with a thermos of coffee and a large protruding wad of dip stuck in his bottom lip. The ground creaked with every step as he approached the group. He was a young guy with a strong jaw, big forehead, and spiky brown, gelled hair.

Watching him with a slight glare, I became agitated just knowing he was going to be part of my Phase One. I watched and watched as he circled around the group, holding the cocky, haughty expression, until he came to a stop. His eyes shifted down to my hands, then over at Tim, and in a sarcastic tone, he asked "Well, well, well, what's this? Is this a Phase One project, Tim?"

"Why, yes it is, Brian." Tim's voice held the same tone of sarcasm. The exchange between the two was tense, and I became more agitated. Looking up at Brian, I watched as he stuck his tongue down in the wad of dip, pulled his bottom lip up, and shifted the bulge from one side to another. With eyes full of uncertainty, he declared, "Well, Tim, unfortunately we don't have time for this presentation today."

"Damn it," I blurted as the anger took control and I tossed the papers over my shoulder.

Brian's eyes shot to me. "Well, apparently we see how Chad feels about his Phase One project."

Realizing my mistake, I immediately stretched back, grabbed the packet and came back to an upright position. I tried to redeem myself, "No, no, no, I just got upset. I just really wanted to present today. Please. I'm sorry."

"Hmm, not sure I believe that," Brian responded.

"No, I'm serious, I promise. I just got a little mad, that's all."

"I don't know, man." He looked over at Tim. "What do you think, Tim?"

Shrugging his shoulders, Tim gave a look of disbelief. *Great. Just what I need.* By this point I could tell they had made up their mind. Resigned, I set the packet down and sat in silence.

Out of the corner of my eye, I continued watching Brian as he slowly and methodically paced around the circle. His eyes were glued to mine. *What is he doing? Quit being a hard ass.* I felt like I was being toyed with, but he finally stopped in front me and spoke, "All right, well, let's see just how important Phase One is to you." *This sounds bad...really bad.*

He asked, "How many logs would you be willing to peel in order to present today?"

I knew it! I knew he was going to throw a bargain out like that. Not sure how to respond, though, I let myself think. *What's not enough to please them but enough to convince them? And what's the number I can handle?* Coming to a decision, a hopeful expression ran across my face. I responded, "How about five?"

Brian rubbed his face, paused, and looked over at Tim. "OK, I think that's fair." Whew. But five logs did not sound fun. *Whatever, it's worth getting out of here. I hope.*

Presenting my Phase One packet felt like a joke. Phase One requires us to say we have a problem with drugs or alcohol. I didn't have a problem. Not me. But I had to play their game, especially if I ever wanted to get out of there. It all felt like a circus act. Lying through my two front teeth never came easier. Or so I thought. Tim read right through me and knew I wasn't sincere, but most of these kids weren't. When you're forced into rehab, chances are you don't think you have a problem. But time away from substances and constant reminders of the negatives will have an impact no matter what. It takes time, but it'll happen. For the time being, however, my thoughts remained engulfed with rationalizations. On the outside I had to remain the star rehab patient. The better I am, the quicker I go home... I think.

Whether I felt like I had a problem or not, it did feel rewarding to accomplish one of the major requirements of the facility. Productivity is a major component of my personality that keeps me happy, but when I was using, I wasn't very productive. I didn't realize it, but not being productive gave me a feeling of worthlessness. It hurt my self-esteem and magnified the depression I always tried to numb.

The facility was teaching us to be productive even if we did not realize it. The work days, the kitchen duties, the treatment sessions— they all resulted in a feeling of accomplishment. Even peeling a log created a sense of productivity. I had not yet peeled one, but I walked out to the pile of unshaved logs searching for the five with my name Sharpied on the butts. Throwing the six-foot logs around like telephone poles, I searched and searched, but could only find one. *What happened to five? There's only one here.* Eventually I came to the conclusion that five was only for effect. Of course it was. Everything around here felt like it was for effect. The whole exchange between the counselors about not having time and this and that must have all been an act. They wanted to see my reaction and that's exactly what they got. Realizing I had been played, I laughed sarcastically. Those clever little counselors. What little brats. It was all a game and they used it to their full advantage.

Not to be outdone, I bent over and grabbed the log by the end, dragging it to the peeling zone. I stepped carefully to avoid the rabbits hopping around the fresh pine strips. Large and fat, the rabbits ate the scraps from behind the kitchen, and the peeling area seemed to be their zone. I guess the freshly shaved pine strips made a nice bed.

After setting one end of the log up on the three-foot rack, I searched for the peeling utensil. It was a boomerang-shaped tool that had two handles and a sharp blade in the middle. Well, maybe not sharp, but at one point I'm sure it was. Years and years of pine sap can only be stripped off so many times, but the blade seemed to work. I had seen many guys strip a log without a problem.

Sifting through the mounds of peeled bark, I found the blade, shook off the stuck pieces of bark and went to town. The handles were freezing but the more I stripped, the warmer they became. I discovered the best method was to stand over the log and pull the blade toward my body. Strips anywhere from a few inches to a couple feet would come sliding off. All together, it took about twenty minutes. Not bad, and I felt productive.

That evening I received an interesting letter from my dad and a letter from my math teacher, Coach Davis. The letter from my dad read:

Dear Chad,

I'm trying to work today at the office, but my mind is constantly going and thinking about you.

It was such a hard decision to get help for you, but all of us know you were going down a path that would lead to destruction and possibly death due to drinking and driving. We all love you so much and even your principal is helping us. He said that if you get three needed courses completed, then you will get a diploma from the school. This will really help as we apply for colleges and I'm happy that you want to go to college.

Remember, this is a big bump in the road for you, but it will pass and things will be o.k. for you and your aspirations.

The lawyer is working on your recent speeding ticket. We are still amazed that you didn't get a DUI after drinking at the dance club and being stopped with 24 miles over the speed limit. Drinking and driving is a deadly combination and when it's mixed with drugs, bad judgment, accidents, and police involvement is inevitable.

Chad, we want you to help yourself to get better and ask that you stay at Wilderness for the program. It's the best thing we could do for you as we love you very much.

Please write or call,

Love,
Dad

P.S. We are of course always praying for you!

Setting the letter down, I became confused about the statement of drinking at the dance club. *How on earth did he know that?* There was no explanation. He was in bed when I got home and he definitely wasn't at the club. Nothing added up, and I was appalled at the thought. I felt like everyone knew everything. All my secrets seemed to be public knowledge. But how? It blew my mind. I thought and thought, but never landed on any possible reason.

The other statement about my principal was also interesting. This was the first time I had thought about what was going to happen to my schooling. School was still important to me and I had to get an education if I ever wanted to be successful. Reading that my principal was going to allow me to finish school and get my diploma was a huge relief. After being shipped off, I had no idea what my future held. This news gave me hope. And boy did I need hope.

The next letter came from my math teacher, Coach Davis, who had been my teacher for the last three years. Over the years I had developed a strong relationship with him and looked to him as a mentor. He was the most spiritual man I had ever met. If there was anyone closest to God, it was he. The letter he wrote went as follows:

Chad,

Life is just not quite the same without you in my math class! (For three years we've been together!) I imagine you will have some stories to tell when you return, but I just want to encourage you to look to Jesus through all this· He not only is our hope of salvation, but he is a source of strength for our daily battles· He can fight (better than any of us) the enemy who wants to destroy us· We have prayed for you many times in math class and though you will miss our math party this week, I hereby extend a special invitation to a special party when you get back in town! Enclosed is your last math test... the highest grade in the class! Take one step at a time, Chad! You know I've been in some difficult spots... but by God's grace we can make it!

With much love,
Coach Davis

The letter sent memories swirling though my head. Good memories, warm memories, comforting memories. It was nice. We had many fun times in all three years of his class. All three years, the class held the same students. Since it was small, we all grew close, becoming comfortable with one another. It was more of a support group at times than a math class. Lindsay was in the class as well.

Later that evening during the recovery meeting, one of the boys read from the opening readings and I actually paid attention. After hearing the words for almost a week straight, it was impossible to continually tune them out. For some reason the words seemed to touch home with me. I'm not sure if it was due to the haze being lifted, the Knees to Knees exercise, or the treatment sessions—or maybe it was a combination of all three—but something was definitely shifting inside. Part of the reading, the most convincing part for me, talked about using something stronger than drugs or alcohol to help keep you sober. To me, that higher power is God of Christianity.

Throughout my life, I had kept a strong faith in God and tried in every manner to do the right thing. However, once I started getting messed up on a regular basis, all of my religious values started slipping away. They did not disappear, but impairment does not share. Now, I'm not saying that one day I tried alcohol and drugs and instantly lost all my values, but slowly my usage continued to push more and more until it eventually pushed everything out of my life. I didn't care about anything: school, family, God, friends, or hobbies. I pretended just to look good, but my effort was not there. I was simply going through the motions.

I once read a passage that talked about how you can only serve one master, either God or some other form, whether it was lust, greed, money, materials, or whatever. Unfortunately, my usage had become my new master. Substances took control of the wheel and took off for a ride. We were swerving down the road, hitting every bump in the way. Even worse, I was always hiding things from my parents, school, friends, coaches, teachers, and family members. It was always a game of deception.

Although I believed that my usage was helping me, which in the beginning it did, it was really causing more stress and grief than I could have ever realized. It was impossible to deal with life on life's terms. Once my head was up in the clouds, I couldn't see anything from the correct point of view. The only way for me to get the correct perspective was to be forced to see it.

The Reunion

Friday came around, which marked the completion of two full weeks at the center. By this point I had become accustomed to the life and had fallen completely into the groove. The center was its own self-regulating state, with its own customs, rules, and rulers. If you didn't conform and accept their ways, then you would have one hell of a time. I realized this right off the bat, but many of the patients did not. But at some point or another, they all eventually came around. You could not survive if you didn't.

The day before, during treatment, we were required to participate in an exercise called a Walk Around. Two counselors sat in the middle of an empty circle of chairs. One at a time, a patient would walk around the outside of the circle. As the patient walked around the circle, he would get drilled with questions concerning his willingness to change. The goal of the questions was to expose each individual's defects and to make them realize why they were here. After this the patient had to actually say the defects and commit to changing. For many of the patients, the questions had to do with changing their physical appearance, which for me meant shaving my grown out, hippie hair. Once the counselors felt you were ready to change, you were granted access to the circle to join the rest of the group. It was not easy. Addicts and alcoholics hate to think there's something wrong with them. Drugs and alcohol keep those thoughts far away. It was a very effective exercise because it relied on peer pressure. Once the first guy entered the circle, he had what everyone else wanted, and he was also allowed to demand answers and pressure the others into changing. For an addict or alcoholic, peer pressure is the best means of demanding change, because peer pressure is the reason many of us first started to use. My first experience with impairment was induced through peer pressure.

I was sitting in a circle with three of my best friends on the back porch of a house. The pressure was tightening around my throat, and the familiar rumbling of anxiety pounded relentlessly through my chest. Less than a year ago, during seventh grade geography class, I had made a conscious decision to never try drugs or alcohol. Being taught all the dangers and dead ends of substances through numerous drug and alcohol courses, I was definitely never going to try that stuff. It's stupid. It's lame. Just say no, right? Sure. Simple enough. Why even bother?

I looked down at a friend's hand, holding a pipe made from an Aladdin genie toy. It was staring at me, provoking me, tempting me. *But drugs are bad. This is the part where I just say no.* Drugs are like a disease and had the pipe not been resting in a hand, it would have looked like a disease. But the hand changed everything. The pressure engulfed me. *What do I do?* Inside my head a little voice tried to speak. *You made a commitment. You can't. This is wrong, bad, a dead end. Just say no.* The tiny voice tried so hard, so hard to speak loudly enough, but the peer pressure spoke louder. Actually, no words came from the boys. There was no coaxing. No comments of "come on" or "just do it" or "don't be a wimp" or "don't be a loser." Nothing. Just a hand along with an expectation.

I grasped the homemade pipe and brought it to my lips. Careful not to catch my eye-length hair on fire, I sparked the lighter and pulled it toward the end of the pipe. The flame sparked and cracked as I breathed through the small hole, pulling the flame over the leafy green substance. The weed caught and the green substance morphed into small strands of smoke. I watched as it floated away. The group won. I was still a part of the group, and that's all that mattered.

No one wanted to be left out of the circle at the center either. It was cold and lonely on your own, like a turtle outside its shell. We all wanted to be part of the group, and this meant meeting the demands. My demands centered on being honest. By this point everyone had figured out I struggled with honesty. Most addicts and alcoholics do. Before being granted access, I had to admit to lying about my drug history and make promises that I would not lie and would admit all lies and struggles to my family during Family Week. The group was going to hold me accountable. This, of course, did not sit well. There was not going to be any sugar coating. My favorite thing, sugar coating. *Damn it.* Anxiety coursed through me.

Being confronted and actually having to admit to my tendencies to lie made it feel more real. When someone tells you that you are not honest, you can easily shrug it off, but to actually say it yourself gives a whole different perspective. Just saying the words aloud can help make your brain accept it. Change was sparking, and it scared me.

The exercise was not easy for anyone. Chris stormed out, cursing and yelling before punting a mini trash can twenty feet in the air. Germ just shut down and left the building. Thomas bawled and bawled about having to shave his head and take out his earrings. A fourth guy just flat-out refused to join. But before the day ended, everyone was sitting inside that circle. It offered comfort, peace, and most importantly, acceptance. All we had to do to join was face ourselves. Sounds easy, but it's the hardest thing for any of us to do. There is nothing worse than facing your defects and for the user, drugs and alcohol mask the defects. So of course, after a life of using, being forced to face the issues brought out some intense emotions. But that's rehab for you. Intense emotions—and it's the only way to change. If it were easy, everyone would do it and succeed.

Before the exercise, the patients were emotionally all over the place. Some were holding grudges, some were in denial, some were angry, some were arrogant, and others didn't know up from down. Walls were up between every single person. We were a mess. No one really knew each other or cared for that matter. There was no group. But the exercise broke us down, publicly exposing all of our defects. Everyone saw everything, and we realized we all had wounds. Pure humility smothered every patient, but compassion spread like a wild fire. No one was better than anyone, and cohesiveness formed when we finally realized we were all in the same boat. A new sense of belonging floated between us. Attitudes were adjusted and grudges were lost. We came together, and from that point on, we looked after one another. Going through an emotional war like that pushes all the petty issues aside. It was beautiful and very powerful!

That Friday was another work day, which ran much smoother than the previous ones. We all had a much better attitude, fewer complaints, and we had no problem helping one another.

Later that evening, after the movie, I spent my time writing back to friends and family. I had received many letters and had written every single one of them back. I even started receiving response letters from the people I wrote back. To each person I wrote, I talked about everything that I had done and everything I was going to do. Depending on the person, the process took about three pages per letter.

I still had not written my mom or dad, though. There were too many mixed emotions associated with them. I loved them, but addiction kept me at a distance. They were trying to help me, but I didn't need help. A wall of defense stood tall. Subconsciously I had to protect my usage and this meant keeping them as far away as possible—and it hurt. Love was there, but it was buried. The only thing I could do to avoid becoming emotional was to not think about them. Just push them away.

Saturday was yet another work day, and the temperature was still frigid. Today we were going for a ride on the flatbed trailer, pulled by a green John Deere tractor. The ride took about thirty minutes before we were out in the middle of the forest.

For the next few minutes we stomped around in the three-foot snow, waiting for instructions. A young guy who looked liked Toby McGuire was in charge. He had a chainsaw in hand and was wearing long chaps covering his legs. He peered around the forest for a few moments before making up his mind and demanding, "All right, follow me." We stomped through the snow about thirty yards until he stopped and instructed, "Here's the plan, guys." He paused to make sure we were all listening—a hard thing to do for a bunch of addicts and alcoholics.

Pointing at the tractor he said, "As I chop down the trees, you are going to drag them to the trailer and pile them up on top of the flat." Not waiting for any comments, he pulled down his orange safety glasses and yanked the chainsaw's cord. The work day had begun. The chainsaw sliced through trees like a hot blade in butter. Every five minutes, he had chopped down at least seven trees. The trees were small, about four inches in diameter and eight feet tall. I eventually figured out they were the trees used for peeling. Then the peeled trees were later used for the fence or bunk buds.

The day was long, cold, and tiring. We broke for lunch and then went straight back to work. It was exhausting. Stomping through the snow was enough to wear us out, but dragging a tree through a forest made it ten times worse. It was repetitive as well. Without a change in jobs for eight hours, my mind wandered. I started thinking about Family Week and all the things that I was going to face. It scared me to death. Up to this point, I didn't have to think about it because it felt so far away, but now it was less than forty-eight hours away. Forty-eight hours! It was too close and the anxious thoughts hovered all the way through the night.

That night, after numerous attempts of tossing and turning, trying to find the best position, I eventually gave up. It was late, probably two in the morning. I sat up to clear my thoughts when I noticed a beam of light shining on one of the bottom bunks. It took me a few squints, but I eventually made out a clear picture. It was one of the guys reading a book with a flash light. Curious, I hopped down, tip-toed across the room, and sat down on the edge of his bed. He was one of the guys who had just come back the day before from the Trip. They had left for the Trip before I arrived at the center, so I had just met him for the first time that day. His name was Dan and he was in his late twenties. The Trip gave him a new perspective on life, but the baggage of his previous life was weighing heavy. He was having trouble coping with all the problems he had caused throughout his life.

We sat there talking for a few minutes before I realized he was reading the Bible. Curious to know if he was a strong Christian or just discovering Christianity for the first time or somewhere in the middle, I decided to probe. He gave a depressed sigh and explained, "You know, man, I've heard of some stories, you know, like Easter and Christmas, but I'm ashamed to admit this is the first time I've actually read the Bible. Honestly, I don't know where to start." My heart went out to him. I knew of a good story to keep his interest going.

During eighth grade my teacher taught a really cool parallel between the story of the Great Flood and the lifespan of humans. I knew he would enjoy it, so I explained.

In Genesis 7:11 of the New International Version of the Bible, it says, "In the six hundredth year of Noah's life, on the seventeenth day of the second month—on that day all the springs of the great deep burst forth, and the floodgates of the heavens were opened."

The interesting part of this passage is the last stanza that talks about the floodgates being opened. It has been theorized that there was a ring of water that sat between the earth and outer space and its purpose was to filter the sun's rays. The theory is based on the Scripture describing the creation in Genesis 1: 6-8: "And God said, let there be an expanse between the waters to separate <u>water</u> from <u>water</u>. So God made the expanse and separated the water under the expanse from the water above it. And it was so. God called the expanse sky."

When the flood came, this halo collapsed to help flood the earth. Once the ring was gone, the sun's rays were not as filtered, creating a more direct, harmful ray.

Before the flood, it was not uncommon for man to live up to nine hundred years old. Noah was six hundred years old during the flood and died at the age of nine hundred fifty (Genesis 9:29). After the flood there was a steady decline in lifespan. The decrease in lifespan was first noted with Shem, who was one of Noah's three sons. Shem was ninety-eight years old at the end of the flood and died when he was six hundred years old, three hundred fifty years less than Noah's age at death. Shem's son, Ar pach'shad, lived four hundred thirty-eight years. Ar-pach'shad's son, She'lah, lived four hundred thirty-three years. His son, E'ber, lived four hundred sixty-four years and his son, Pe'leg, lived to two hundred thirty-nine. Four generations later, Te'rah gave birth to Abraham (Genesis 11:10-26). Abraham died at the age of one hundred seventy-five (Genesis 25:7).

As I finished explaining, the look on Dan's face was of complete wonder. "Hmm, that's actually really cool, man. So people lived that long... That's nuts. But the whole declining age thing makes perfect sense. Thanks, dude, that helps." His enthusiasm was contagious. It helped fuel my little fire of faith that had almost been drowned by the taste of alcohol.

For the next hour we continued with other forms of discussions about the Bible. Years and years of Christian schooling had ingrained in me tons of knowledge about the Bible. He had so many questions and I helped answer as many as I could. The flame in his heart was growing, and a believer was being born. A new higher power was taking control. It was exhilarating.

The next day was Sunday, the day before Family Week started. I had dwelt so long on the idea of Family Week that I had finally come to terms with the fact that I was going to have to share a lot of heavy things. So instead of worrying, I decided to enjoy the recreation day by focusing my attention on the rugby-style game that Wilder Andy had created. The game was exhausting. With heavy boots on, we stomped through the snow like a bunch of out-of-control idiots. It was quite a sight, but we were smiling, laughing, and working as a team. It was a blast and helped keep my mind clear. To me, learning to have fun without using was crucial to my recovery. In the past, everything I had done revolved around getting high or drunk first. I had lost my drive to be active. But I loved being active. All my life, I enjoyed sports and games. It wasn't until I started using that my drive to be active slowed. Substances just seemed more fun. And substances don't share.

After the long, fun, stress-free day came to an end, we all retreated to bed. Physically worn out, I decided to go straight to bed. As I lay on top of the quilt, staring at the yellow-colored plywood ceiling, I began thinking about the Trip. Family Week had been pushed aside and the next nerve-wracking obstacle would be here before I knew it. The Trip. It did seem exciting since I had a strong sense of adventure and tons of experience camping through Boy Scouts, but after seeing the frostbitten fingers and hearing stories of unbearable conditions, I was still nervous. Camping in the snow was a foreign idea, and my mind started playing out different scenarios of the possible things that could happen. First I envisioned four feet of snow, a blizzard, and piercing thirty-mile-per-hour winds. I pictured my entire face covered with a ski mask, sunglasses, and a hat, attempting to block the winds but having little effect. I imagined my face covered in frost and burns, and envisioned my desperation as the counselor demanded we press on. I thought about falling into a stream, getting hypothermia, and losing my fingers. I pictured a ski breaking and trenching through the snow the rest of the trip.

Fortunately, as quick as my mind created the negative scenarios, another part convinced it to stop. The conscious and analytical part of my brain convinced my anxious and creative side to quit worrying. It was getting me nowhere and only making things worse. I thought about the positive sides of the Trip. Having a strong liking for the outdoors, I knew it would be fun to get out in the middle of nowhere and see God's most vivid creations, snow-covered mountains. With this in mind, instead of envisioning treacherous conditions, I pictured myself with a smile, admiring the power of the snow-covered mountains mixed with the serenity of the frosted evergreen trees. My face absorbed the sun's rays without a hint of wind, soaking in the euphoric image. A warm feeling filled my soul. This thought eased my tension and took away the stress. Finally I felt tired and my body convinced my mind to relax. Quickly slipping into random distorted thoughts, I fell asleep.

The next thing I knew, the fluorescent lights illuminated a few feet from my face. I sat up and found myself still wearing clothes. After a couple slow rubs on my eyes, I gazed around the room to see a few people already up, dressed, and ready to go. At first it seemed odd, but then it all made sense. Family Week was beginning today. These kids were more nervous than a cat in water and most likely didn't sleep an ounce. I slept like a baby and was excited to see my family. The feelings of anger, bitterness, and distrust had faded— only because my addictive side was shrinking. I could feel love again, but I was still nervous.

Sliding off the edge of the bed, I hit the floor with the usual thud and hopped in the shower. For some reason, the shower that morning felt unusually refreshing. With my arms pressed against the wall, I let the warm water flow down my back and performed a few breathing techniques to help clear my mind. It helped soothe my nerves. Today was going to be intense and I at least wanted to start off right. After a fifteen-minute shower, I felt stable enough to jump on the emotional roller coaster. Family Week...

After dressing, I made my way to the dining hall. In the distance, I saw the snow-covered field filled with cars. This changed everything. Actually seeing evidence of my family being on the ranch was overwhelming. It wasn't the fact that I hadn't talked to them since I'd been there; it was the idea of having to tell them all of my dark secrets that sat so tight in the middle of my chest. But there was nothing I could do. Trying to convince myself that everything would be fine, I joined the line for breakfast.

It was apparent that everyone was clearly agonizing over the same thing, and the mood of the line was not its usual happy-go-lucky style. Everyone kept to themselves and, for the most part, no one said a word. When one guy expressed his concern about seeing his parents, no one attempted to give him any advice. We were all scared. Everyone was too consumed in their own thoughts to even entertain the idea of helping someone else. I was no exception.

After breakfast, we stood nervously at the front windows just staring at the Treatment House. That's where our parents were. The parents were in a meeting to prepare them for the day. I could not even begin to imagine what the counselors were telling them. It was beyond me. So instead I patiently waited, trying not to think of the horrid look they were going to have in a few hours when I rattled off my extensive laundry list of drug usage.

Peering out the windows felt like an eternity. Waiting. Waiting. Waiting. The sun was out and there wasn't a cloud in the sky. The temperature had gone from the frigid zero degrees to the low thirties. At the beginning of February, a hint of spring was beginning to show its face. I never could have imagined that low thirty-degree weather would feel somewhat warm. Growing up in Georgia, thirty degrees felt like hell was freezing over. And if it happened to snow, the entire state might as well shut down. Schools closed, people missed work, and all the kids tried to make snowmen from one inch of snow in Atlanta.

Time crawled by and the anticipation was killing me. With every passing minute I became more anxious. *Come on. Come on. Just come out. I can't take this.* Another five minutes passed. Then five more. *What is going on?* It felt like they were never going to come out. My eyes were glued. Still only silence. No movement.

Finally! The doors opened. My nerves exploded into high alert. *Here we go. Oh man.* Despite the anxious feelings, joy managed to sneak in. I wanted to see them. I loved them.

We all waited. No one moved. Not until they saw their family. Only then did a boy walk out the door. For the most part, each boy would greet his family with warm embraces and giant smile. After a few families filed out, I saw my brother, dad, and mom.

My parents were both wearing giant yellow ski jackets and my brother was wearing a beige snowboarding coat. I waited a few seconds as they came closer. My mom usually stands out in a crowd due to her unusual height of five feet, eleven inches. Her hair is highlighted blonde, styled above the ears, and her blue eyes shine like a star. At this moment, the sun was bouncing off the snow, lighting her up like an angel. She is slim and long and usually carries a happy expression. But today her face showed only signs of anxiety.

My dad walked next to her, hand in hand. His Italian-style black hair naturally grew up and toward the back. His eyebrows are dark and as bushy as a caterpillar. He carries a businessman's belly, but not enough to hinder any physical capabilities. His olive skin maintains a natural tan throughout the year. He is only about two inches taller than my mom. And at that moment, his facial expression matched hers. Anxious.

My brother, Matt, who is about the same height, has short brown hair with a slight wave. It is usually gelled, but today was different. His hair was light and fluffy. I guess he wasn't trying to impress anyone. His eyebrows are just as bushy as my dad's, but more of a brown color, matching the color of his eyes. His face, slightly rounded, normally carries a jolly, personable expression, but not today. Another anxious expression. I could sense the anxiety dripping from their pores.

Unable to take the anticipation any longer, I flung open the door. The cold mountain air smacked me in the face. Staring right at them, I walked with my head held high. There was a giant smile smeared across my face, but none of them were making eye contact. Confused, I walked quicker. I practically ran into them before their eyes made contact and lit up. My mom spoke first, exclaiming, "CHAD!" I immediately embraced her, holding her tighter than I had ever held her. She buried her head in my chest and completely lost it. The warm tears pierced through my shirt. Surrounding the two of us, my dad and brother joined in. The emotions were too much. They both broke down. I broke down. It was overwhelming. As I cried, the anxiety and fear came crashing down. Practically melting into the snow, I felt the love penetrate every ounce of my body. Tears streamed down my cheeks. No one could speak. We just cried.

It must have been at least a whole minute of embracing before my dad slowly released and stepped back. I slid my hands off my mom's back and she peeled her face off my chest. She looked up with red eyes, wet eyelashes, and a giant smile. "Oh, honey, I love you, I love you! You look so good!"

Her warming voice shot chills down my spine. It made me quiver, but I smiled. Despite the tears and sniffles, I managed to say, "I love you, Mom."

I looked over at my dad. He was nervous, but still looked happy. He stepped closer, grabbing the sides of my arms and looked me in the eyes, "Hi, son. How are you?"

Nodding my head up and down, I smiled as a stray tear slid down my cheek. "Really good, Dad, I feel really good." That was exactly what he was looking for. His eyes swelled up and the overwhelming emotion tool control. Two tears slid down his cheek, stopping at the creases of his giant smile.

I slid my finger across my eyes before turning to my brother. Holding out his arms, he cracked a giant grin. "Come here, big guy." I stepped forward and embraced him. It was a quick hug. He pulled back, slid his fingers across his eyes and looked straight at me. "Good to see you, brother, so good to see you."

Acknowledging his statement with a smile, I responded. "You're telling me, man. You are surely a sight for sore eyes." My brother was my rock and was always there to tell me exactly what I needed to hear. To finally see him in person made me feel ten times stronger.

The emotions eventually released their grip and my dad switched the tone by looking up at my hair. "Jeez, I didn't even recognize you with that hair. Looks good." I reached up to touch it, remembering the shaved head.

It all made sense. *That's why I practically ran into them before they acknowledged my presence. The hair...* I responded, "Yeah, I was wondering why you guys didn't see me sooner. I mean, I saw y'all from a half mile away."

Glancing over at my mom, I noticed she was staring at me. She couldn't take it anymore and reached out to give me another hug. I let her hold on as long as she needed. Once she finally released her death grip, I asked, "Well, you guys want to take the tour?"

"Sure, yeah, OK," all three of them responded at the same time.

I instructed, "All right, well, follow me, but step carefully," I pointed down at a few different icy patches. My dad reached out, grabbing my mom's hand, and off we went taking small, cautious, baby steps. We went down the carved path of snow that led to the shack. The porch creaked louder than usual as the weight of all four of us stepped across the boards. I slung open the crooked door and we all ducked, crossing under the rotting doorframe. Taking a moment to glance around, the three soaked in the cold air, admiring the game tables. My mom pointed and spoke first, "OH, a weight set, perfect!" I couldn't help but laugh a little bit at her enthusiasm for an ancient set of weights, but agreed that it was better than nothing. Once they were done looking, I led them across the creaky porch, through the snowfield, and over to the dining hall.

Reaching down toward the knob, the door flung open and almost hit me, stopping at my boot. It startled me for a second. I looked up with a split second of anger, but when I saw Germ's smiling face, my fumes simmered down.

"CHAZZ," he exclaimed. "What's up, man." Looking back over his shoulder, he declared, "Hey, man, these are my parents." They both stepped out from behind. His dad had a full grayish-brown beard and thick glasses. His mom had dirty blonde hair with matching thick glasses. I stuck out my hand.

"Nice to meet you guys."

His dad spoke, "Same to you, Chad. We've heard much about you."

In return to Germ's introduction, I looked back at my parents and repeated the process. We chatted for a few moments before Germ and his parents left the dining hall and I continued the tour. My dad glanced around, slightly nodding his head while mumbling "Yep." He clearly approved, so I moved the group to the cabins.

This time I let them walk in front. They stepped up the five wooden stairs, crossed the porch, and into the cabin. I was curious to see their initial reaction, so I remained quiet. Standing at a distance, I watched as they strolled through the cabin and quickly gazed around. My dad did his usual look of approval. My brother said, "Sweet! Not too shabby." He looked over with a smile. *Yeah, well, it looks a little bit nicer when you're a guest and not a resident.* But I didn't want to ruin the mood, so I remained quiet.

After they had seen it all, we worked our way back to the front porch of the dining hall, where several of the counselors and other families were already waiting. I looked across the field and noticed a few other families still wandering around. Carsten announced, "All right, patients and family members, we're going to hang here for a few minutes. Once everyone's back I'll give further instructions."

While we waited, I glanced around at all the families and patients, assessing the reactions of the reunion. The majority of patients and families were happy and chatting casually, but there was one family that just didn't seem too thrilled. I stared at this family for a few moments trying to figure out why the grim looks. The patient of the family was a heroin addict named Bran. He was a nice guy, fairly quiet, and respectful toward others. Physically, though, the heroin had clearly taken its toll. The dark circles and bags below his eyes were a strong indication of the usage. But his hands and arms told the real story. They were spotted up and down with black circular dots from missed needle attempts, leaving permanent mole-looking scars. His eyes also helped complete the story. Looking into them felt like looking though a dark glass window. There was so much pain, so much hurt, and so much defeat. His expression was worn and tired as he came off of the physical addictions. After seeing a repulsive sight, such as the bottom of the trash can, he would rush out the back door, barely holding back the vomit. Most people might get a little nauseated, but his body was so unstable from the withdrawals that the mere sight was enough to send him tossing his cookies.

This was also not his first attempt at a rehab, hence the unenthusiastic reunion with the family. My heart went out to them. Their pain was illuminating. It almost made me feel unworthy of being in the same place. I felt lucky that my path never reached that point. Was it only because my path had been intervened? I don't know. I had definitely tried some of the harder drugs, but never heroin.

Impairment from other drugs distorts decision making, and the right context could have sent me swirling down that heroin spiral. It scared me for a moment. But whether I did a hard drug or a more socially accepted drug, I was starting to believe that all substance abuse leads to death. Some deaths just come more quickly than others. Death by substances does not have to be grounded to a physiological definition though. It can be defined in ways like death in the individual, death in relationships, death in spirituality, death in life in general. In my opinion, once the individual is living for the drug, he or she is dead. I've heard family members talk about their loved one being hopelessly addicted to drugs or alcohol and the family member crosses his arms, looks away and says, "She's dead to me."

For a moment, I was completely lost in Bran's situation. Hurt and pity consumed my thoughts. Not that he wanted pity, but I couldn't help it. The next thing I knew, Carsten's voice shot through my thoughts, "All right, family members and patients, the time has come to begin the treatment day."

At the sound of his voice, the blissful mood deflated like a flat tire. In a blink of an eye, expressions turned from relaxed to serious. My anxiety jumped. I knew I was not the only one, but having allies wasn't going to help my situation.

Family Week Part One

The whole crowd inched its way over to the Treatment House. The slow, cautious pace made me feel like I was walking the plank as we baby-stepped our way into the building. The worn, musty carpet smelled unusually strong. I noticed a piece of paper on each door. The paper to the left had my name listed along with Bran, Germ, Chris, Thomas, and two other guys. This was the group for the week, the group for the Trip, and the group for the execution.

A few minutes passed and all the families had finally shuffled in, sitting in the circle of chairs. No one wanted to be sitting in that circle. The anxious and fearful looks were as clear as day. People shifted from side to side, looked down, or tried to have a small conversation. There was an attempt by some brave soul to lighten the mood, but it went nowhere.

Carsten poked his head in from around the door, took a glance, and disappeared. I was ready for him to come in and begin. *Come on. Come on. Let's get this over with. I can't take it anymore.* He never returned. Instead, Mike, the counselor from the Knees to Knees exercise, strolled in. His full brown beard, thick eyeglasses, and annoyingly calm expression were back. *No! Not him!* I almost belted out a few derogatory words, but my nerves were too focused on other problems. Mike closed the door behind him and sat in the only empty chair. Once again, his lack of words didn't change. He slowly gazed around the circle, like a creepy Chucky doll. It was dead silent, and my mind was racing. *Not the pauses, anything but the pain-staking pauses. Please no... Why me? Not again! Like Family Week wasn't bad enough, now I have to deal with this again.*

With my eyes glued to him, I waited and waited and waited. He reached up with his right hand, stroked his beard, and finally spoke, "Well, here we are." *What?! That's it! That's the best you could come up with?* I let out a sigh and slumped. *This is going to be a long day.*

Some people were looking down, shuffling their feet and nodding. Others looked stunned, some looked scared. My dad looked straight at him, slightly nodding his head, and my mom gave a fake smile. Matt did nothing. He wasn't even going to pretend this was going to be fun. I just blankly stared until Mike finally spoke again. He gave a summary of what the day held. I was relieved when he said the parents would leave after lunch. *Thank God!* Apparently, one treatment session of family time was more than enough. I looked down at my dad's gold watch. Ten o' clock. *OK, not bad. Only two hours, I can handle this.*

Mike finished the introduction and declared, "Today will revolve around the drug history of the patients." *Oh man... The drug history. This is it! Show time...* I was extremely anxious, but I was done dragging my lies around. My drug history had been lying too heavy on my chest and I could not wait to throw it off. Mike looked around the room and asked, "Who would like to start?" *Here we go.* I was ready and started to raise my nervous hand. Out of nowhere, Germ blurted, "I'll start." *No, no, I had just mustered up the courage.* My hand fell back by my side as Germ began. He ran through his history fairly quickly, but I tried to pay more attention to the expressions of my parents. I wanted to try to predict their expressions after I completed my history, but their bland expressions weren't helping. Germ's parents' looked much the same. It confused me. I expected more emotion. More looks of horror. At least some yelling or something. Nothing. Just neutral. *Were they too stunned to respond? Was it too much? I don't get it.*

Germ finished and Mike asked for another volunteer. I shot my hand up and declared, "ME, I'll go." Acknowledging my words, Mike gave me the floor. I looked over at both my parents. Their expressions were neither anxious nor eager, just sort of blank. My mouth opened, but the shame prevented me from maintaining eye contact. Instead, I looked down, shifting my brown boots from side to side, and started with, "Well, Mom and Dad, I want to tell you that I have done more than just drink alcohol and smoke marijuana." My heart rate jumped. *Did I really just say that?* It was too nerve-wracking and my mind seemed to detach from my body. The part of my mind that likes to hide things completely panicked and must have checked out. It was now standing in front of me in complete awe, but my mouth continued moving, "I've done cocaine, Adderall, mushrooms, GHB, Ecstasy, and a variety of pills."

BAM! It was out, it was over. I looked up, but they did nothing. Not a word, not a mad expression, not a verbal scolding, nothing. Just stillness. *My brain raced. Am I supposed to say more? What else can I say? What do I do?* I went blank. Finally, someone said something. It was Mike, "Now doesn't that feel good?"

My eyes went to him. Relief washed over as a smile formed on my face. "YEAH! Wow, it feels amazing!" I quickly turned back to my parents. They were both smiling. No way. I couldn't believe it. They were actually smiling. My mind and body flooded with endorphins. All that worry and stress for nothing. It looked like that's exactly what they wanted to hear. I realized they didn't care what I had done; they just wanted me to be honest. That's it, nothing more, just solid, clear honesty, and boy did it feel so sweet. I stood up and they immediately stood up. We embraced and I practically melted with relief.

A few moments later, we released the embrace and they looked up, smiling. We returned to our seats, but my mind urged me to say something. I wanted to say that I had only done some of the harder drugs a couple of times. I wanted to downplay the list, but right as I started to speak, I remembered a valuable lesson. Never try to minimize what you have done; by attempting to minimize, you will only lose respect and your credibility. I had done what I had done and there was no changing it. So I kept my mouth shut. My expression turned light and I looked over at Mike. He looked proud. "Well done, Chad. Great progress." The attention mixed with the compliment forced a giant smile, but I quickly looked down. Attention was never my thing. I responded with a simple "Thanks," and the next thing I knew, all attention was off and Mike was asking for a new volunteer.

Whether it sounds like a big deal or not, admitting to anything that an addict or alcoholic has kept hidden is crucial for recovery. Addiction's best friend is deception. Deception is what allows the user to keep using. Deception lets the user convince himself/herself and other people that everything is fine. The more the usage increases, the more the deception has to increase. It's a positive correlation clear as day. Just like in the movies: The best con the devil ever played was convincing people he doesn't exist. Deceiving oneself or others into believing the issue doesn't exist is the devil's best trick. You have to see the problem before you can solve it. Acknowledging a problem is the first step in recovery, but getting to a point where you accept there is a problem is the biggest battle of all. Many people don't see the problem on their own. It's too hard, the call is too strong, and using is so precious. It offers too many good things. Therefore, protection for the usage is necessary and deception is how you protect it. Something has to intervene. An outside perspective can help, but just telling a person they have a problem is worthless. Even showing them they have a problem is worthless. Maybe for a second there will be a moment of clarity, but it won't last. Users have to feel it for themselves. They have to feel it from within. They have to taste it, and honesty is a great start. Coming clean with anything kept hidden will give the user a taste of what honesty feels like. No matter who you are, honesty feels better than deception. Again, addiction and honesty don't share. If honesty is present, addiction will go latent.

My parents tried for years to convince me I had a problem. Whether it was drug testing, speeches, drug counselors, psychiatrists, or just rubbing addiction-related mistakes in my face, they tried everything. Their last and final attempt came from a forced meeting with a recovering addict/alcoholic. He was a young guy, only a few years older than I was, probably in his early twenties. I didn't even know about the meeting until he was standing in my parents' doorway. Coming down the stairs to investigate the door bell ring, I was confused by the visitor. *Who is this guy? What's going on? Great... He's here to talk to me.* My mom introduced him as Scott. Being respectful, I shook his hand. He claimed we were going for a ride. *Maaaan...* It was so awkward and I hated awkward feelings, but there was no choice. It was too late to blow him off, but at least he seemed like a cool guy. We hopped in his small pick-up truck and drove to the nearest coffee shop. I was actually surprised about the way the conversation went. He didn't try to preach, he didn't try to tell me I had a problem, he didn't even really mention my usage. All he did was talk about himself and this Wilderness program that had saved his life. *Wilderness program? That sucks. I'd rather not. Being stoned and drunk is way more fun.*

Overall, the meeting went well. He was trying to be my friend, but he lived a different life than I did. A life without substances, and it sounded terribly boring. When he dropped me off, it all went in one ear and right out the other. A freshly rolled joint helped erase the conversation. Perfect.

For the next hour and a half I rested easy, watching other patients squirm as they went through their drug histories. One of the patients brought more to the table than just his history. Something was sitting too heavy on his conscience. The patient, Chris, ran through his history like it was nothing, but right when it sounded like he had nothing else to say he dropped a bomb. Chris calmly looked at his parents. "Oh, by the way, did I tell you guys I stole a few cars?" *What! No way had he just said that.* I couldn't believe it. It wasn't the fact that he had stolen a few cars. I mean, that's not rare in a rehab. No, it was the way he said it that blew everyone's mind. He might as well have been saying, "Oh, hey, by the way, you want to grab a bite to eat later?" Even my jaw hit the floor.

Everyone else in the room stood still, waiting for a reaction. Chris's dad let out a small, dumbfounded laugh while his mom took off her designer glasses and rubbed them with her shirt. Finally his dad, with a slight smile, shook his head. "No, Chris, I think you must have forgotten about that one." The room erupted into laughter. It was priceless.

In the middle of the laughs I could hear Mike say, "Never a dull moment in recovery, right folks?" Even my parents were laughing. It was actually nice. The mood of the room had been so serious and intense that a good laugh brought a second wind to the group.

Twelve o'clock eventually rolled around and it was finally time to break. The session was brutally intense, but it was over and everyone was extremely relieved. Despite the roller coaster of emotions, there was no doubt everyone was feeling better. Smiles were everywhere. We had all made steps to recovery—honesty—and there is nothing harder than for a habitual user to speak with honesty. It just plain hurts. Usually the things they are hiding are hidden for a reason. Mainly because the user knows whatever they are hiding is going to hurt that other person. Tissues littered the room, but it felt good. The smiles, hugs, and body language told it all. A warm feeling floated amongst the group. There were numerous walls broken down and the possibilities of healthier relationships were forming.

As we broke from group, everyone strolled over to the dining hall to enjoy a warm wholesome lunch. The chef served spicy chili, hot rolls, green beans, fresh fruit, and layered brownies. The comforting meal only reinforced the positive mood. It was nice to share a meal with my parents, and even better, to share a light conversation. We certainly had enough emotional distress for one day and just wanted to enjoy each other's company.

After lunch my parents and I stood on the porch enjoying the moment until Carsten announced it was time for the parents to leave. Before they left, my parents asked if I needed anything. Of course I had a list. I told them to get some protein bars, a rubber cord to work out with, and Reese's peanut butter cups. Ever since I had been at the "Dub," I couldn't get enough sweets. The chef always cooked a fresh dessert and I never passed. Apparently when you quit drinking alcohol, your body tries to fill the void with sugar. Alcohol turns into sugar extremely easily and once you take that away, well, your body craves sweets. Maybe that's why I was craving sugar or maybe it was just the surge of endorphins when the sugar hit the taste buds. Who knows, but one thing was certain-I couldn't get enough sweets.

I said goodbye to the Family and waved as the car went bumping down the snow path. Once they were out of sight, I walked back to the cabin to catch a moment by myself. The treatment session had worn me out and I wanted to take a break. My bed seemed to be the best spot. I swung up onto it and let my mind debrief. It was amazing how the emotional stress could take so much energy out of me physically. I felt like I had been playing an all-day sporting event. My eyes were heavy and I gave in to the tired glaze. There was no resistance left in me.

DING DONG, DING DONG, DING DONG. My eyes tried to open and my brain tried to make sense of the noise. It took a few blinks before I realized what was going on. *The bell, that terrible bell. Oh how I hate that bell.* It was demanding my presence, but my body begged not to move.   Realizing worse things would happen if I didn't get up, I forced myself off the bed, stepped out into the light, but my eyes could barely open. The combination of sticky contacts mixed with reflecting sunshine forced my eyes closed. It was extremely unpleasant.

Eventually reaching the front porch of the dining hall where the bell was located, I joined the circle of guys and we waited for everyone to appear. The bell was used for several reasons: to wake up for breakfast, to call a meeting, to confront an individual, or to address an issue. So far I had only seen it used for breakfast. Since it wasn't morning, I could only imagine. Carsten stood next to the bell so I figured he had to be to one who rang it. As we waited, Carsten asked, "You all right, Chad?"

"Fine," I responded, staring at the ground. "Just woke up from a nap."

With a hint of attitude, he responded, "That's what I thought."

Great, this better not be about me.

When everyone was accounted for, Carsten began. "All right guys, I feel like the first day of Family Week went really well. I want to say how proud I am of all of you guys for being honest and making great progress. There is nothing easy about what you guys have done today and I feel like you should know that."

He paused for a moment, looking down from the porch as smiles ran across the group. I think the smiles were more relief than his words. The bell was always nerve-wracking. Even if we were in the middle of taking a shower when the bell rang, we would have to jump out of the shower and go straight to the bell. Sometimes guys would be wearing nothing but a pair of sneakers and a soggy towel. Their lips would almost turn blue from the cold air.

He continued, "So, as a reward for your good work, we are going to have an hour of free time before starting back into the afternoon session."

This pleased the crowd. It may not sound like much, but to have an hour cut off the three-hour afternoon session was nice. Everyone was toasted after the first morning, and at this point, the less treatment the better.

Carsten finished his speech. "All right, guys, go have some fun."

As the group started to break, Carsten interrupted, "Wait, guys. One more thing." We all turned back to face him. "No sleeping during the day."

The comment was obviously directed at me, but he didn't say anything else and just left it at that. I couldn't have cared less anyway. After that morning session of Family Week, everything else seemed like small potatoes.

The next morning, we were back in the circle. Everything was the same as the day before except two chairs sat in the middle of the circle. They were intimidating and I could only think the worst was yet to come. Anxiously, I waited for the counselor to come in. The anticipation was building again. My dad sat on my right, my mom on my left, and Matt was next to my mom. My dad fidgeted in the chair, my mom had a blank stare on her face, and Matt looked out the window, probably dreaming of a beach. I, on the other hand, couldn't stop staring at the chairs. They were so calm, so quiet, and so harmless. Just sitting there, doing nothing.

My perception was not harmless, though. My mind twisted the chairs into thoughts from hell. Honesty equals hell and those chairs were screaming honesty. Those thoughts made me miserable and I started to squirm on the inside.

A few agonizing moments passed before Mike walked in and shut the door. I felt trapped, like he put a steel bar over the door. Nowhere to run, nowhere to hide. A feeling of helplessness came over me. No one was on my side. Just me, here to face my previous actions, and Mike was the regulator. It reminded me of court, but without the bailiff and the fancy bench.

I watched Mike carefully. He strolled around the circle, handing each person several sets of papers. He reached me and dropped the papers in my lap. I swallowed and read the sheets.

Three Positive Things About_____
1._____
2._____
3._____

Three Negative Things About_____
1._____
2._____
3._____

Three Things You Regret You Did Toward This Individual
1._____
2._____
3._____

Unsure of what to make of the sheets, I waited for Mike's instructions.

"All right, folks, today is a Knees to Knees exercise."

No way! Not again! I couldn't believe it. *Again! AAAAH!*

Mike continued, "Each patient will fill out one sheet per family member. Each family member will fill out one sheet for the patient."

Mike paused, letting our thoughts marinate. Then he continued. "Each family member will meet the patient in the middle and touch knees as you take turns reading your sheet."

He looked around the room. "All right, any questions?"

There were no questions. Everyone was too nervous. "OK then, I'll give you fifteen minutes. Once everyone's done, we will begin."

My eyes shifted down to the sheet and I immediately went to work. Writing. Writing. Writing. Filling out the sheets was no problem. I had so many things on my mind. My dad's sheet took no more than a couple minutes and my mom's was the same. There were so many things to say, they just came pouring out. My brother's sheet took a few extra minutes, but I was done long before they were. Not unusual, though. Everything I did was at a fast pace. A fast pace... part of my impulsiveness. Part of my usage.

Fifteen minutes later, Mike scanned the room. Instead of asking for volunteers, he pointed at Bran and declared, "All right, Bran, let's do this." Bran slowly stood up, fixed his pants, and walked to the chairs. His dad followed and they both sat down. I watched as they shimmied and scooted until the chairs were close enough for their knees to touch. Bran took a deep breath and let out a depressing sigh.

The process took about twenty minutes. It was intense and emotional. He laid it all out, but his dad remained skeptical and quiet. Nonetheless, it was tear-jerking. Except for the sniffles, the room stood silent. Walls were crashing.

Bran finished the process with his mom and dad, and began with his eleven-year-old brother. By this point the little guy had watched his older brother bring himself to near-death experiences more times than he could count, but this was the first time he had been brought to one of the recovery centers. The emotions were too strong, too strong for anybody, and the pain flooded the room.

The second his brother started reading, he started bawling. It was unbearable to watch someone so young agonize in pain.

Once the two did finish the process, the whole room was sniffling. Between the sobs and cries, the little guy kept saying, "I don't want you to die, I don't want you to die…I can't live without you." There were piles of tissues scattered throughout the circle, and I wondered if this place got a discount on tissue orders. Two more days of this and we would all be buried.

As Bran and his brother sat back down, no one said a word. There was really nothing that needed to be said. Mike allowed the silence to sink in. Sometimes quiet is more powerful than anything a person can say. For this moment, silence was impeccable.

When Mike spoke again, he was quiet, almost at a whisper level, as he asked, "Who would like to go next?" I was definitely not ready after that show. My emotions were already on the edge of boiling over. To make it through this, I needed to be collected and in line. Instead of raising my hand, I stared at the floor, avoiding any persuasive movements from my family members.

After what felt like an eternity of silence, Germ volunteered to go. Germ and his family went through the same agonizing process, but it did not have nearly the same effect on the audience. Germ and his family finished, but it took so long that it was time to break for lunch. I realized that this family session would be an all-day occurrence. That did not sit well.

After lunch and a full stomach, I decided it was time for me to get the exercise over with. Not like I had choice, but I had come to terms with it. I had been stressing out all morning and even more during lunch. My mind was so wrapped up in the fear of the unknown that I could not concentrate on the harmless conversation bouncing between my family and me. It was like I was on autopilot. I would respond, but my response was not creating a two-way conversation. Instead, I would just base my response more on their behavior and tone of voice than the actual meaning of their words. The majority of my thoughts were off dancing through the stressful field of the unknown while the rest were barely holding the minimum parts of the conversation.

A few minutes after the lunch hour, the entire group was sitting back in the circle of death. I was desperately hoping that Mike would not point at someone to go, but instead ask for a volunteer. I was determined to start the process. To my satisfaction I heard Mike ask, "So who's going?" Instead of raising my hand, I immediately stood up. There was no way I would let someone else go. I had to do this. By standing, I figured Mike couldn't deny my attempt.

Walking toward the chairs, I looked over toward my parents, debating with whom to start. The debate didn't last long. The anxious but eager look streaked across my mom's face called out to me.

"Come on, Mother," I offered my hand toward the chair. "Please join me."

Fortunately, the mood in the room was light. After the good lunch break, I could tell my mom was anxious but not stressed, and I felt better.

But the moment she pulled her chair close and we touched knees, something happened. It was like a wooden spike of shame was plunged into my chest. All the memories of yelling and cursing at her hit me right in the heart.

Forcing my shame-filled eyes upward, I met my mom's loving blue eyes. She didn't say anything. The love in her face was like a needle poking my heart. With my guard finally down I could feel her love still just as strong as ever. She would never give up on me and it felt good to know that. But the shame, the shame was crushing me. I couldn't take it any longer. I had to get it out. My eyes fell to my sheet and I started.

"Mom, you are the most amazing mother I could ever ask for. You love me unconditionally and I can't thank you enough for that. Thank you for always supporting me and standing by me no matter what."

Quickly glancing up, I tried to read her expressions. She had a look of appreciation, love, and gratitude. It felt good, but knowing the worst was yet to come, I could not enjoy it. My eyes fell back to my sheet. I looked at the second section of the three negative things. The lines were blank. I realized that there was nothing negative I could say about her. Anything I could think of was so petty compared to things I had done that I couldn't even begin to call them out. I looked up and slightly shook my head from side to side, saying, "There's nothing negative I can say. You have been the most amazing parent and I don't have any right to say anything bad. I don't deserve anything you've given me."

Her expression changed to a look of pity and she replied, "No, honey, you will always have my love, no matter what."

My heart broke, my shame twisted and pulled. The overwhelming amount of guilt cut deep. It was so amazing that she could say something like that. After all the pain I caused, she still said that! A tear swelled and I couldn't hold it back. A couple went sliding down my cheek. I was too choked up to talk, so I paused. One tear dripped off my chin, splattering the sheet below.

Pulling myself together, I looked down to the next set of statements. These were going to be the hardest, and based on my emotional state, I knew these would be the end of me. Taking a deep breath, I let out a quivering sigh and started.

"Mom, I regret yelling at you. You don't deserve that. I regret not listening to you when all you were trying to do was help me." I paused, trying to fight back the emotions, but my mom waited for the last regret. Completely choked up, I tried my best to muster out the most painful regret I had left.

"And most of all..." Sniffle. "And most of all, I regret not returning your love."

Plunge, the stake of shame sunk all the way in. My eyes swelled and the tears flowed, streaming down my cheeks, off my chin, splattering one after another on the sheet. That was it. Everything was out and I was overwhelmed with shame. My head hung weighted with guilt while agonizing moments crawled by.

All of a sudden I felt the tips of warm fingers on the bottom of my chin. My mom pulled my head up to meet her eyes. Her facial expression was full of pity and empathy. She stood up and so did I. We embraced. No words, just an embrace. She held on tightly while I wiped my tears.

A few moments later, my emotions came back under control. My mom released her hold and we sat back down. Relief washed over me. The quick release forced out a big sigh from my chest and it felt fantastic. I felt like I had finally done what I needed to do, and I was on the way to becoming the person I was proud to be.

It was brutally hard to admit to my wrongdoings, having to directly tell the one I hurt so much that I was sorry, but once it was over, the feeling was indescribable. I could feel our relationship reconnecting. It had been broken for so long, but all it took to mend was admitting I was the one wrong. That was it, nothing extravagant, no special promises, no crazy acts of love; just a few simple statements, a few apologies.

It was now my mom's turn to go. By this point I was ready for whatever she had to say and I sat quietly, intently listening. "Chad, you are so special to me and mean more to me than you will ever know. I cherish you with everything I have and my only wish for you is to live a happy, spiritual life." Her eyes fell to the sheet for a brief moment while she read what she had written. She looked back up.

"You have an amazing heart and care for people like I have never seen. You are a great listener. And you are such a blessing."

Instantly a smile from ear to ear ran across my face. It was such a relief to hear her say positive things. I had been so concerned that I had damaged her thoughts to a point of no return, but with those words I quickly realized her love was truly unconditional.

As her eyes fell back to the sheet, her tone changed to stern and authoritative.

"Chad, the manner in which you have treated us is not good. You need to get your priorities back in line. Your lack of respect for others needs to improve."

She was right and I knew it, so I nodded my head in agreement. She stared straight at me, but I didn't say anything, just acknowledged her eye contact. Carefully analyzing her expressions, I waited for the final section. She looked down at the sheet, but this time her eyes only came partially back up. She paused, looking down toward the ground. I couldn't figure out what she was doing or where she was looking. I waited. She looked up at me, batting her eyes. Pause. She sighed and looked up at the ceiling as a tear slid down one cheek. She raised a curled index finger up to her lips. Another tear slid down the opposite cheek. Seconds passed. Her tears pierced my heart and my eyes swelled again. Her pain. Her hurt. Her agony. All caused by me. The thought was unbearable, but she finally took the finger away and spoke.

"Chad, I regret not knowing how to help you." She hurried to the next statement, fighting back the persistent tears. "I regret not spending more time in trying to help you."

The emotions caught up. Too choked up to talk, she was forced to pause. Her nose sniffled and her lip quivered. She looked away, trying to push it back down. It took a few moments, but she started to speak. Her whispering voice quivered, "And... most of all... I regret... waiting until now to do something about it."

Her eyes flooded with pain and my heart broke. Her red-rimmed eyes were as cloudy as a dustbowl. The tears were streaming, but she gazed directly into my eyes. All I could feel was pain and it was killing me. This look was created by me and I couldn't bear the thought. Immediately standing up, I pulled her into my arms and squeezed as tightly as I could. She sniffled and sniffled and sniffled, and her tears pierced my shirt. I whispered, "Thank you, I love you so much."

Continuing to hold her, I waited until she stopped sniffling. It wasn't until then that I partially released my hold. Still in my arms, she looked up with red eyes and a tear-streaked face. She smiled, I smiled, and it felt good—painful, but good. Everything was out in the open and we knew each other's hearts.

We both looked down at the same time. Her tear marks had created a wet face across my chest. We both started laughing. At this point, the emotions were all used up and only laughter could exist. It was a tremendous relief. Our connection felt complete. Full of a newfound life. It was just what the exercise was meant to do, and it obviously worked to the full potential. My mom slowly turned and walked back to her seat as I sat back in the hot seat.

I looked over toward my dad and nodded. He reached down to the floor, picked up the sheet, and headed my way. The knot in my chest tightened. *This is going to be worse.*

My relationship with my dad is different than with my mom. Not in a bad way, but different. Dad was more concerned with me doing the right thing. He of course loved and cared for me, but he wanted me to succeed. Not be a screw-up like I'd been. Dad was the one who kept me in line. Nonetheless, he still showed love.

Dad cautiously sat down, his eyes glued to mine. My heart rate increased, continuing to beat faster with every passing second. Motionless, I watched as he reached down on the sides of the chair, grasped the metal legs, and shimmied his way close. As our knees connected, my throat closed. I could barely swallow. *Here we go again.* My emotions had just been drained, but here came round two.

Normally he would be the first one to speak in a situation like this, but this time I was the one in the spotlight. It was my show and

I was the one expected to do the talking. He just looked at me with a blank expression, waiting to hear what I had to say. My mind raced, my nerves pulled me in different directions, and all I could think about was how much I had disappointed him. Fearing his possible reactions, I panicked, trying to think of excuses for my behavior. He was the one always in my way, so he was the one I always lied to. Lying was my best defense, and after years of practice, it came naturally.

A strange thought shot through my brain. A foreign thought. Honesty. I actually remembered the feeling. *Honesty. Honesty. Come on, Chad, be honest. It feels so good. Remember? Just be honest. That's all it takes.*

No. That's a terrible idea. Don't be honest. Honesty hurts. Don't say anything.

The little voice tried harder. *HONESTY. You have to. NO MORE LIES.* My dad's eyes were waiting. They screamed honesty.

My new conscience, combined with his glare, won. It wasn't about hiding anymore. I had been ducking and dodging for long enough. Now was the time to step up to the plate and let it roll. There was no way I came this far not to repair myself and start a new life. The old me was like a crusted shell. It was thick, but every day I was in Montana, layers were shedding. No way was I about to kneel down and start picking up the bits and pieces of my old degrading habits. It was nerve-wracking, but I made up my mind. *I have to be honest, completely honest.* More than just what I had to say. There were other secrets I needed to get out. Secrets only I knew. *I have to tell him. I have to be honest.* Honesty pulled my conscience to life.

"Dad, before I begin I want to get honest about something." My eyes fell to the floor. I couldn't take his stare, but I continued to speak. "I want to tell you that one night in the neighborhood, I was driving a friend's car and wrecked it into a curb. The axle blew out and I barely got the car back to her house. It cost several thousand dollars to repair. She told her dad that she did it."

There, I said it. That's good enough. No need to say I was drinking. What will he think? It'll be terrible. You can't say that. Wait! Honesty. What's the point of saying it if it's not the whole truth?

The debate continued. Again. There were two sides battling for control, but only room for one. Honesty or deception, sobriety or impairment, life or death!

Life or death...deception is the culprit and honesty must prevail.

"I was drinking as I wrecked the car."

Bam! It was out. I said it. *Wow! I did it.* Honesty came in and took a seat. It felt great and I was shocked. *Me, honest?* It was scary, but I felt clean. That was it, the whole secret was out and I no longer had to protect it. The secret was exposed and the burden was lifted. My eyes sparkled with serenity. It felt wonderful!

Still nervous about his reaction, though, I looked up, expecting the worst. To my surprise, he held no angry expressions. It wasn't happy, but it wasn't mad. His face actually looked neutral. I was a little unsure about how to interpret his reaction, but there were too many other things on my mind to dwell on it. Either way, whether he reacted negatively, positively, or neutral, all that mattered was that I was being honest, no longer hiding behind closed doors. The gap between me and my family was shrinking. Every honesty hurdle I leapt, I came one step closer to a true healthy relationship.

Before I spoke again I looked at my dad. A small smile was forming. It felt so good not to be hiding that I took a moment to soak it in.

After the brief moment, I decided I was ready to go on. This was the easy part, the part where I got to tell him how great he is. Maintaining eye contact, I started speaking.

"Dad, you have been the best father I could have ever asked for. Your overwhelming amount of undying support and love is beyond describable words."

I glanced down at the sheet for a split second then back up. My first three statements came out as a blend between the three positive statements and a thank you.

"Thank you for being supportive no matter what. Thank you for loving and caring for me, despite the way I have treated you. Thank you for standing by me and always being on my side."

His expression stayed the same. No smile. No surprised look. Just steady and serious. He spoke. "That's why I'm your father. I will always be there for you, Chad, no matter what."

The words shot chills up my spine. They stabbed me in the heart and the shame felt heavy. I had to pause for a moment before going on. I fought back the emotions and was forced to look away. My eyes swelled with tears.

Once I leveled out, I was ready to tell him the same thing I told my mom. I stared back into his eyes and spoke, "I have no room to even begin to tell you anything negative after the amount of support you have given me. I'm the one in the wrong here and I don't have anything to tell you except thank you."

Leaning toward me, focusing on every word, he nodded his head. Before I started to speak, my shame pulled my eyes down.

No, Chad. Look him in the eye. Face your pain. Don't escape. By this point, facing pain was not so foreign. I was getting used to the intense emotions. Normally I would sugar coat everything, but it just softened the blow. Negative emotions made me squirm, and I liked things to be happy and smooth.

This part of my personality was definitely part of the reason I liked to use. When I wasn't sober, everything was numb. Any negative feeling could go numb with impairment. I could be in a conversation that picked, criticized, or brought my actions to light, but I would just zone out and wait to go light them into the air or drink them away. I didn't deal with issues or problems. In my mind, there was no reason to. Life was supposed to be fun and I expected to skate through it.

Finally, after clearing from the haze, life was coming into the real perspective. It wasn't about avoiding negative and awkward emotions. No, those feelings are all part of life. Instead, it's how you deal with them that truly matters. I was finally realizing that life wasn't a cakewalk, and every time something came up, I couldn't go hide behind a substance. My ability to deal with the negative issues was improving only because I was forced to feel the awkward feelings. By exposing me bit by bit to real emotions, I was getting a new perspective and slowly realizing the awkward feelings weren't the end of the world. They weren't fun, but they weren't as dreadful as my mind played them out to be. Family Week was the ultimate test. Here was my chance to truly taste awkward, negative feelings. I was becoming stronger, more confident every time I claimed my actions. All I had to do was step up to the plate. The next plate was staring right at me. It was my father and I took a deep breath, holding eye contact. There was no reason to look at my sheet. The regrets I held were stitched deep in my heart.

"Dad, I regret taking your advice and throwing it in the trash. I regret taking everything you do for me for granted. And most of all, I regret not being the son that you have taught me to be."

My face went blank. Everything I had been holding deep inside was finally out in the open. The amount of relief was so intense, my mind couldn't comprehend it. There was no stake of shame, no surge of endorphins, no feeling of guilt, and no joyous parade. Just blank, neutral, bland. My body had nothing left. My emotions were as dry as a bone and everything shut down. Not focusing on anything, I stared off into the distance. The room was quiet; no one moved a hair. The moment was for me and my dad, and everyone respected that. I had said everything I needed to say and just waited for a response.

"Thank you."

My vision refocused and I looked him in the eyes. "You're welcome." I smiled from ear to ear, and he returned the same expression. It felt great.

He reached down to his sheet. It was my turn to listen while his eyes fell to the sheet. A few seconds passed and I waited until he looked at me. With a painfully calm and collected voice, he started speaking.

"Chad, you have so many positive qualities... I struggled with which three were the best, but these are the ones most important to me. Your compassion for people is remarkable. You always put forth a great effort in everything you decide to do. You have a great character and sense of integrity."

I immediately smiled, looking back at him. It was nice to hear him say positive things. After dwelling on my mistakes for the past two days, the positive comments were the only thing keeping me going. But the feeling only lasted seconds. His eyes fell back to sheet. The negatives were coming and his voice became stern.

"Your lack of communication with us needs to improve."

This statement caught me off guard. Not that it wasn't true, it just wasn't exactly what I was expecting to hear. It took a second but I figured out what he meant. One of my flaws is that I tend to lock up when I am confronted with something. Instead of responding by defending my position or agreeing with a confrontation, I would just stay silent. This had been going on for most of my life and would greatly frustrate my parents. But it was definitely a problem that kept me using. By not dealing with issues straight up, I was more likely to go use to numb the negative emotions.

After allowing the first statement to sink in, he moved to the second.

"You need to be a part of this family again."

Another accurate statement. My eyes darted around the room, analyzing the statement. For the past few years I had slowly withdrawn bit by bit from the family. It didn't happen overnight, so I didn't really realize it until this moment. Before I had started down this path, our family would operate as a whole unit and not as separate individual parts. But once a part of the group breaks off and goes its own way, the group is no longer a group. The other members have to overwork to hold at least part of the cohesiveness together. It isn't fair to the rest of the group, but I couldn't have cared less. By going off on my own, the family struggled. Even the relationships that didn't directly involve me suffered. The stress affected the relationship between my mom and dad and also between my brother and my parents. It wasn't right or fair. As I realized I was the one damaging the relationships, a new wave of guilt swept over me. It hurt, but my dad was starting with the third negative comment.

"You must quit treating your family with no respect."

Ouch. My heart bled as I mulled over the three comments. But the fact that my heart even bled was huge progress. If I had heard these comments back at home, I would have thrown them in the trash and disappeared off on my own. My heart had crusted over and any comment bounced right off.

I was changing. My crust had shed and my heart was out in the open. It was vulnerable to any penetrating comment. That is what made this week so important. This was Family Week and this was the time to change. Today was meant to bring issues to light and make steps to correct them. Change is hard, but this was working.

One section remained and I was curious to hear what my dad's regrets were. This section seemed to be the most painful, but in a different way than the negative comments. These comments hurt the most because they were raw, focusing on nothing but love. By this point there were no grudges left, no anger, no other feelings that stood in the way. Just love. This section basically summed up all things that hurt the most as a result of the patient using. All walls were broken and feelings of frustration or anger had already been brought to the table and dealt with in the proper manner. Only love remained.

My dad looked down at the sheet. I could tell he had already read what he wrote and must have been thinking about how to start. I calmly waited. He raised his eyes. Before speaking he didn't take in a deep breath or let out a sigh. He didn't shuffle his feet or shift his weight. He didn't avoid eye contact or glaze over. He simply stared straight at me, and it pinched my soul. But his eyes held pain. Pain I was not used to seeing. I knew it was hard for him. Hard to say what he was about to say, but he did it anyway. His mouth started moving and his words came from deep down.

"Chad, I regret not spending more time with you. I regret having to send you here, I feel like I should have done more to prevent this." He was starting to get choked up. His words were trailing off, clearly fighting something back. It hurt me. These emotions were simply contagious. Watching him choke up felt like a nail was being hammered into my heart. It was so weird seeing him express heavy emotions. It cut into me. His look of stone cracked and he still had another comment to go.

He attempted to say the last statement, but stopped. The area around his eyes turned deep purple mixed with a bright red. It looked like his heart was twisting and tearing in a set of vice grips. A few moments passed before he finally cleared his throat and threw out the last comment.

"I regret not knowing more about your usage."

Plunge! Again! My heart twisted and ripped right in half. My compassion went streaming out to him, but I was too choked up to tell him how wrong he was. It wasn't his fault. He knew plenty about me. He was such a good father, and there was no reason for him to take the blame like that.

His expression was blank and cloudy, his eyes glazed with pain. He was experiencing an overwhelming sense of guilt, but for no reason. Knowing my words would only come out in fragments I decided to just stand. He immediately rose and we embraced. More tears slid down my cheek. The embrace was strong and it lingered.

Releasing from our embrace, I noticed he had a few tears. He immediately wiped them, looked at me, and smiled. Our connection was back. Every frustrating, agitating, grudge-filled moment was gone. It had all been crushed, smashed, and demolished. All that remained was raw, true love uniting and glowing between us.

Family Week Part Two

I sat back down and my dad returned to his seat. There was one person left to go, my brother. I reached down to pick up the next sheet, but Mike's voice made me pause. He was looking at the wall clock.

"You've got about twenty more minutes, Chad."

I rose up with the sheet clasped in my hand and my brother walked over. For a moment, I thought Mike was going to cut us off.

I ran through the positives, negatives, and regrets. The process was not nearly as emotional as with my parents. The one thing that was hard for me, though, was to tell him how sorry I was for the incident that occurred between us in Athens, Georgia. Other than that, we both had a few different things that had been sticking between us, but just like with my parents, after bringing them to the surface, they were gone.

In order to close the day, we all circled up with our arms around each others' shoulders and recited the serenity prayer. "God, grant us the serenity to accept the things we cannot change, courage to change the things we can, and the wisdom to know the difference."

I may not have recognized the importance of the serenity prayer then, but now it is ingrained in my veins. There are so many things in life that need to be accepted, but at the same time so many things that need to be changed. For all my life I had never truly tried to change anything. I was content with taking whatever path seemed the easiest, which was totally against what my parents taught, but it's just the way I was, I guess. This made change that much harder and there is nothing easy about making a change. We are all creatures of habit and naturally fall into a pattern of routine, but positive changes are what can make you feel alive. For the first time in awhile I felt alive, and I would never go back to change a single moment that day at rehab.

As the treatment day slowly came to an end and the brutally intense emotions released their grip, there was no doubt everyone was exhausted. But there was a magical, positive vibe fluttering around. Into the retiring sun, the patients and families piled out the front door with looks of joy and serenity. Some had their arms around each other's shoulders, some were hugging, and some were just joking and laughing. It was quite a sight to see all the broken relationships holding new life. I was no exception and walked with my arm around my mom's shoulder while my dad and brother were joking lightly next to me. The setting sun sent golden rays bouncing off our faces, heightening the feelings of the day. We felt whole again, like the way a family was meant to feel, and it felt absolutely wonderful. There was no pain, no frustration, and no awkward fake conversations. The loss of the fake conversations was the best part. In the past, the fake conversations were the only way we got along, but without having to hide my usage, I could talk openly and freely with them. We could even joke about some of the dumb things I had done. The conversation was stress-free, full of life, and it felt great.

My family and I chatted for a short while before it came time for them to depart. I waved as they hung their heads out the windows and bounced down the snow-covered path. After losing sight of them, I let out a sigh and strolled over to take a seat in the rocking chair in order to debrief. I was emotionally drained and it was taking its toll on my body. With a clear conscience for the first time in years, I actually enjoyed the serene moment. I let the back of my head rest against the wooden chair and gazed into the horizon with no purpose. In an ocean of colors, the swirls of red, orange, and yellow were cast across the snow field. The silhouette of the mountains mixed with the pine trees stood above the field. I took in a deep breath of the fresh, clean, undisturbed mountain air and let out the biggest sigh of my life. All the feelings, emotions, and energy came pouring out, but my body was left in the rocking chair as I went for a trip across Serenity Mountain.

The next morning I woke before the lights turned on. I felt like a different person, like I was reborn. It wasn't more than a couple minutes later when I heard Willie's scratchy voice echoing through the cabin, "Rise and shine, boys." But for the first time it didn't irritate me. I felt like a new man and slid off my bed like a kid on Christmas morning. Family Week was half over and I was ready for the day. Of course, I went through the normal morning routine, but today it just seemed to float by. I was not the only one enjoying the moment. Another guy hummed a happy tune while two others were already joking. No one ever started joking that early. There was not a soul in that place who had not been dreading Family Week. Now, it was half over. It was hard to get to that point, but there is always pain before it gets better.

After breakfast I greeted my family with a warm smile and a hug for each one. They had smiles smeared all over their faces and I couldn't help but feel the rush of endorphins flooding me with happy and warm feelings. It was fantastic. What was even more fantastic was that today was not going to be spent in the Treatment House. Instead, we were going out to the obstacle course. I had no idea what that entailed, but as long as we weren't in that house I didn't care. We could have been making snow angels for all I knew, but I would not have been complaining.

Once everyone had gathered on the porch, Carsten, Mike, and another counselor led us out into the woods. We stomped through the soft snow at a snail's pace because the family members were not used to the unpacked snow and it was clearly taking its toll. Some of them complained, but this place is all about enduring pain—even for the family members. Forty-five minutes later, we reached the course and half the group was exhausted. A few moms and a couple dads had to take a seat as they huffed and puffed, trying to catch their breath. I found it amusing, but kept my thoughts to myself. Carsten gave the group a few minutes to catch their breath, but not long; they weren't here to cater to anyone. The patients weren't the only ones that could use their cage rattled. I mean, a good reality check never hurt anyone. Several of the parents were so rattled by the two days of Family Week that they made public commitments to quit smoking cigarettes. It is likely they have tried to quit before, but I had a feeling they were going to do it for real this time. This place is powerful.

Carsten raised his voice loud enough for everyone to hear as he pointed over at two ten-foot beams sticking straight out of the snow about ten feet apart. Tied between the poles were several ropes that were twisting and turning and retied to each other in the middle. The ropes created about thirty different uniquely shaped spaces. "OK, guys, the goal of the exercise is to pass each person through the holes safely on to the other side." The crowd nodded like no big deal. Cracking a smile like he was about to enjoy the next statement, he raised his voice. "However, here are the stipulations. Each person has to go through a different hole and if at any time someone touches the rope, you have to start completely over."

The crowd became uncertain with the challenge. Looking up toward the top spaces, it seemed impossible to get someone hoisted up eight feet and through the holes without touching the ropes. It didn't matter how we felt toward the situation. We didn't have a choice. So we brainstormed. Numerous different opinions and methods bounced around. We finally started after deciding to throw the lighter people through the top. It was working and we squeezed three people through until the fourth person grazed the rope and the whole game reset. We tried the same method again and failed again; another attempt and yet another failure. Forty-five minutes in and nothing but failed attempts and frustration. It was aggravating to put forth so much effort and to get nothing out of it. Eventually we tried a different technique: send people through the bottom to help conserve energy. The change of methods helped the group's morale. By sending more people through, we felt like we were getting closer to the end. Then when it came down to getting people through the top, we failed. Failure for this method was devastating. Our efforts had way more energy invested. You could see the looks of defeat spreading like a cancer.

After two hours, people had just about had enough. Sighs and grunts echoed through the woods. It didn't matter though. We had a task and it had to be accomplished. Two of the patients took control and began motivating the parents to pull it together. "Come on, guys, we can't leave until this is done. Come on, think! Don't give up!" How odd it was to see an addict/alcoholic motivating the team. What a change. There were really good characteristics lying below all those years of terror. Something just had to pull them out.

We changed methods and started sending one through the top and one through the bottom. The stronger and taller guys hoisted several through the top, but waited toward the end to go through on their own. A few of the less helpful people were picked up and passed through the middle. It eventually came down to two guys going through two different, but equally challenging, middle spaces. We had never gotten this far. The thought of failure just wasn't an option anymore. Everyone held their breath.

All eyes were glued as I took in a deep breath, pulled the middle of my pants tight, and slowly lifted one leg up. It was shaking as I methodically placed it through. The rope was too high to place my foot down on the other side. I bent my grounded leg and sprung forward. It was awkward. I toppled over, sinking into the snow. Unsure if I made it, I shot my stare back at the rope. It was dead still. What a relief! The group clapped and some hollered. It wasn't over. There was one person left, and it was going to be the hardest task yet. Chris would have to run and dive through a hole almost the size of him. The margin of available error was so minimal that I began to think it was not possible.

Everyone stood silent as Chris backed up. One mom couldn't take the anticipation and buried her head in her hands. It was going to be ugly if he didn't make it. My eyes stayed fixed. I had to make sure this happened the way it was supposed to. To start the run, Chris pulled one arm back and thrust one knee forward. It looked like he was running in slow motion as every step sunk in the light powder. Snow flew in all directions, his feet flailed and his arms pumped. Like a tiger pouncing on its prey, he pulled both arms back and launched them forward while jumping for his life. His head and shoulders passed through the hole, but he didn't have enough momentum. To compensate, he tucked his chin, spinning into a flip while pulling his legs in tight. His boots were the last thing to go through and I cringed as they tried to slip by. Chris disappeared into the snow. *Did he do it? Did he? Please... Wait. Yes! He did it!* The crowd erupted in shouts of joy and relief. The rope sat motionless. He had done it!

Finally, it was all over. Everyone was ecstatic. One guy stomped over to help Chris up out of the snow. Chris smiled from ear to ear as he brushed the snow off his head and face. Even he couldn't believe he made it.

Carsten came over, sporting a congratulatory smile and said, "Great job, guys. Well done." He looked down at his watch with a smile and commented, "Well, two and half hours later, not bad."

The parents anxiously laughed. Carsten waved both arms in a circular motion and instructed, "Come closer, guys, and form a circle." Once the circle was formed Carsten spoke again, "All right, well done today. Go ahead and give yourselves a hand." The group lightly clapped and Carsten continued, "As you guys clearly experienced, that was not an easy task." Everyone nodded and muttered different words. Carsten kept talking, "Well, you can all relax, because that was the end of the obstacle day. But I want to discuss the benefits of the exercise." People sighed in relief and expressions turned light.

Germ raised his hand and spoke, "I feel like we really came together as a group during a truly frustrating scenario. It was extremely rewarding when we finished."

Chris raised his voice, "Yeah, I agree. And also it felt really good to put in a ton of effort and not give up. I definitely felt like I earned every bit of it."

"No kidding," I spoke up. "The best part about it was the amount of teamwork required to achieve the goal. It was nice to know that everyone was in it together and we were all there to help each other."

Carsten stepped in and asked, "Good, so how can all this relate to your recovery? Family members, feel free to chime in."

My dad raised his voice, "Showing these guys how important teamwork and family support can be was a huge part of this exercise. Without support and love from the people close to you, recovery can be next to impossible."

Chris raised his voice again, "In the past I never put good hard effort into anything. I would usually just take the easier route." He chuckled before saying, "Which was usually illegal." The crowd laughed but he quickly became serious. "After seeing the payout of hard persistent work, I feel much more motivated to go about doing things the right way, even if it does end up being a pain in the ass."

A few other family members commented on the improvement they had seen in everybody in the last week. They expressed how the obstacle course was the glue to the week and pulled everything together. Others discussed the amount of change they had seen in their loved ones and how wonderful it was. Thomas, the young guy with curly brown hair, even raised his voice and talked about how his mom had changed as well. He smiled up at her and announced, "My mom has made serious commitments to change some things about her own behavior." His mom smiled, a bit embarrassed, but that didn't matter. Everyone had been embarrassed at some point. It's all part of change. That was the great thing about Family Week, everyone benefited.

It wasn't just about the patients using. Issues intertwined between family members were equally important. Many times a patient consistently used because of issues on the home front. Family Week was the cure for these issues, but it was going to take dedication to maintain these changes. Change is difficult, but maintaining that change is even harder. The obstacle course helped challenge people and helped them realize how much work was needed to maintain the changes.

After the discussion, Carsten thanked everyone for their undying efforts and declared Family Week to be officially over. Everyone cheered, clapped, smiled, and hollered. We had done it! It was over. No more emotionally agonizing conversations, no more brutally painful admissions, no more three negative statements, and best of all, no more grudges. It was the hardest thing I had ever done, but there was not a single person that skated peacefully through that week. Family Week held no bias—it affected each and every individual.

Tears were shed, walls were broken, relationships were mended, and new beginnings were created. You could not ask for a better ending to a week that held so much nervous anticipation, but it was time. The end had come. Everything that needed to be accomplished was accomplished, so we stomped our way back through the woods until we reached the facility. Knowing the day was complete, the hike felt like nothing. Upon reaching the facility the family members who suffered so much on the initial hike seemed to be just fine. It's amazing how much positive thinking affects an individual.

Before it was officially time for the family members to leave, the counselors gave everyone fifteen minutes to say our goodbyes. In front of the dining hall, my mom, dad, brother, and I stood in a circle lightly chatting. It was so nice to have a harmless conversation that held no negative emotions. We felt whole again. I had always loved my parents, but drugs and alcohol just don't share. With all that in the past, the mended relationship could be seen as clear as day. The body language, smiles, and cheerful conversation told it all.

I looked over at my mom. She gazed at me, smiling, with a look of pure joy. All she ever wanted for me was to live a happy, healthy life and now she could actually see that becoming a reality. Returning the smile, I reached out to give her one of the biggest hugs I had ever given her. Dad was next and I embraced him in the same manner, then my brother. As Matt hugged me, he whispered, "I'm so proud of you, Chad."

With a smile, my dad chimed in, "Exactly, we are all so proud of you. You are really doing good. Keep it up and learn as much as you can out here, OK?" His eyes were confident and loving.

The compliments caused me to look down for a moment, but I quickly pulled up and spoke, "Thanks, guys. What a week, right?"

Sighing a little, my mom responded, "Oh yes, honey, but it was well worth it." My dad agreed and my brother nodded his head. We were all smiling from ear to ear, but it was time. The counselors made the announcement that family members needed to go. I gave each one a last hug and my mom said, "I love you." They all turned their backs and walked to the car. I waved as they drove off into the horizon.

Suddenly realizing it was all over, chills trickled through my body. On the front porch of the dining hall, I plopped into one of the benches as the whole week flashed before me. Resting my head against the wall, I took it all in. A feeling of wholeness consumed my soul. It was a feeling I had never felt. A feeling that the relationships we created were here to stay. I had officially dropped the weight of the resentments, broken down the walls of anger, and faced the issues lying on top of the mountain. With the sun shining brightly against our backs, I put my arms around my parents and we walked around the mountain.

Trip Preparation

With Family Week over, the attitudes of the group had done a complete one-eighty. Instead of anger, vengeance, and hostility, we were cheerful, content, and open to treatment. Family Week had been the cure for our poor attitudes. Before Family Week the majority of the patients were just going through the motions. There was no true effort and certainly no true commitment. Sure, our words may have sounded like we were willing to change, but the body language and the looks in people's eyes told the real story. For so long we had all been caught up in our own self-destructive behavior, there was no chance of convincing us to change. We had to feel it in order to know that sobriety and serenity are out there. Addiction is a disease of acting on feelings.

Accustomed to the dark feelings that accompany a life full of substance usage, our feelings, emotions, and attitudes had been calloused with pain, agony, and resentments. All we knew was that the substances eased the pain. But really they were creating the symptoms. It's a vicious cycle. The paradox of using substances to treat symptoms that are created by that very same remedy is absolutely insane. That's the problem with addiction, and getting out of that cycle is difficult.

For me and many others it worked like this. You start out using for fun at a party or with friends, or even to help loosen up in anxious situations. Everything seems wonderful and harmless for a good while. The substances are a miracle and it could be months before the usage loses its innocence. During that time, though, your mind and body become programmed to expect the substance as a method of release and relaxation. By the time you experience repercussions from using, it is too late. Your mind knows the substances as a form of escape and tells your body to use in order to escape the pain, but pain comes in all forms—emotional pain, relationship pain, legal pain, or many others. Pain does not discriminate. Pain is pain and we think the substances are the remedy. So here we go off into the merry-go-round of substance abuse and addiction. We use for fun, we experience problems, and we use to treat the problems. The substances lose the "just for fun" mentality and turn into a necessity. Once you are running in this hamster wheel, all hope is lost.

And here is where the real problems are created. A life full of usage becomes a life full of problems. Undoubtedly it affects everyone around you. It's not just the user who experiences the pain. It spreads like a cancer into the lives and relationships surrounding the user, but users become too calloused to care. Our substance is number one and everything else will just have to wait. Our loved ones start to take this personally and can't comprehend how powerful the call of the substance can be. They just think that the user cares more about the substance than the relationship. That's not true, though. The call of the substance is just too strong to simply say "no thanks." It's everywhere and all it has to do is whisper into your ear to pull you in. All it takes is a bit of coaxing and off we go running, running, running, getting nowhere, but pulling everyone down.

The cycle spins downward, and over time we get farther and farther away from the original path we were once on. Eventually we are so far from the path of sobriety that we cannot even comprehend the idea of not using. We can't imagine it, we can't feel, and we certainly can't taste it. That's why it is next to impossible to simply tell someone to change their ways. The person must want to change before even beginning to work toward a goal of sobriety. That's why the first phase to recovery is to declare you have a problem and to actually accept you have a problem with substances. Not everyone reaches that first step on their own accord, which is OK. But in order for it to stick, the user must have a willingness to change.

Many of the patients did not have the initial willingness to change. I certainly did not, but once I felt the "other side" by experiencing what it felt like to not carry the baggage of burdens, to not be impaired, and to have that feeling of peace, I was ready to carry the rest of myself over. Family Week gave us all a strong taste of what life was like on the "other side," and it looked great. The majority of us were all so sick and tired of being sick and tired—we were all so tired of running in the hamster wheel. Without being forced to see what life could really feel like, it was too hard to imagine it. We were all too far gone to pull ourselves up above the water. Luckily, Family Week had yanked us out of the wheel and thrown us into the fluffy world of sweet-smelling pine chips. Our eyes were big and full of wonder, and we were ready to explore anything other than the steel wheel that had been holding us captive.

The behavior and involvement of the patients told it all. Instead of having to force the patients to talk during sessions, we were practically fighting over who spoke next. Smiles were no longer a rarity and anger seemed to be extinct. The group was strong, the cohesiveness solid, and we all shared one common goal: to change our lives.

Phase Two of the treatment facility was a more personal phase that required the patient to find something that would get in the way of a life of using. It can be as simple as a sport or as complex as a religion, as long as it comes between you and using. During Family Week patients were expected to work the second phase and pinpoint that higher power. For some, their family members were their higher power. But my higher power, the God of Christianity, was who I could rely on. I would need more power than I could create on my own to carry me through the battle I will be facing for the rest of my life. I will always struggle with substance abuse. I will always have to make a conscious effort to control my actions. I will always need that second voice to counter my initial urge to dive back into a world of empty promises. If I rely solely on my tricky, sneaky mind, then all hope is lost. That is why Phase Two is so important. You have to first realize you have a problem and then find something that can give you the correct perspective. The call of addiction might be a whisper, but it echoes through a microphone, drowning everything else out. Still, to have something that can whisper into my other ear could save me from a world of turmoil and agony.

It eventually turns into a full-blown battle. Addiction is on one side with infinite men and on the other side is sobriety with only a handful of men. It feels a lot like the Battle of Thermopylae between the three hundred Spartans and the unending wave of the Persian army. On my own I would get crushed, just like the Spartans would have been had they not had the protection of the Hot Gates. But with God as my fortress, I could make subtle steps to push and stab my addiction back bit by bit. It would take time and effort, but with my fortress in place I could stand to fight. As long as Addiction didn't betray me and tell Alcohol that there was a secret pass on the other side of the mountain, I'd be fine. That secret passage is where my triggers lie, and at this point I didn't even know what my triggers were. For the time being, I just needed to keep fighting.

With Family Week in the past and Phase One and Phase Two completed, it was time to move on to Phase Three. Phase Three requires the individual to let go of all his old ways. This step can only be experienced and not forced upon an individual, but the Wilderness facility did the best they could to create a feeling of letting go.

After another full week of treatment, instead of starting the work day on Friday, Wilder Andy and Counselor Bill took Germ, Chris, Thomas, Bran, Ken, David and me to a four-hundred-foot cliff to experience Phase Three. Andy secured long climbing ropes around two monster trees and launched the rest of the bundle off the side. As we waited for the setup to be complete, I stared off the edge, admiring the view. For miles and miles all I could see were mountain ranges, pine trees, snow, and the horizon. It was a peaceful sight, but the realization of going over the edge was more powerful. It was a good feeling, though. I was nervous, but at the same time adrenaline gave me that out-of-body feeling. In order to accomplish phase three, everyone had to face their fears and go over the edge. That's what this facility was all about: facing your fears and conquering them.

It took about thirty minutes before the set-up was complete. We all gathered in a circle as Andy demonstrated how to tie the harness. I took hold of a long green strap and carefully tied it. Andy checked it, clicked on the carabineer, and ran the rope through. Before clearing me to start, his normal goofy tone went serious and he instructed, "Now remember to stop halfway down so you can do your Phase Three." Too nervous to talk, I nodded my head. The pile of rope ran from the ground up through Andy's harness, around other ropes in the two monster trees, back down toward me, through a metal figure eight, around the left side of my body, and back up my right side. The tail end of the rope, on my right side, controlled how quickly I fell. To stay at one point, I used my right hand to bring the rope up directly in front of me. To fall quickly, I pushed the rope away from the right side of my body.

I looked over my shoulder and baby-stepped toward the edge. With my heart pounding and adrenaline flowing, I stepped carefully in hopes of not slipping on the small pebbles of the step decline leading to the edge. There was no need to rush and I definitely did not want to fall. At the edge I leaned back, squatting like I was in a chair. Fear numbed my body and my breathing stopped as I transitioned my right foot from the flat horizontal surface to the vertical rock surface. Next came my left foot and I was over the edge.

Squatting into the rock, I exploded off and released the rope out to my side. I had to be twenty feet away from the wall and I went falling, falling, falling. A split second later and I was pulled back toward the wall. Pulling the rope back in front, I stopped falling and zoomed quicker into the wall. My legs absorbed the impact and I pushed off. Again, I fell. It was such a rush.

Halfway down the mountain, I stopped, as instructed and dangled two hundred feet from the ground. I looked up and noticed Bill's face peering over the edge. To intensify his voice, he cupped both hands around his mouth and yelled, "OK, Chad, go ahead."

I looked up at the sky and yelled, "I am deciding to turn my will and my life over to the care of God!" With that I threw out my arms and let go of the rope. My heart skipped, my body dropped, but I did not fall. Andy caught me.

Hanging for a few seconds, I soaked in the feeling of trust before I grabbed the rope and bounced all the way down. I landed like I had been jumping on the moon. The whole experience gave a natural high. That's what I lived to feel, and a natural high felt so clean and pure.

The next day, instead of having a work day, Chris, Bran, Germ, Thomas, Ken, Dave, Andy, Bill and I went to the equipment building to start packing for the Trip. Our mood was light and joyful because we were packing and not working. The Trip was the final phase of the center, and we all yearned to not be at a treatment facility. Conquering the Trip meant leaving the facility.

The packing process was no small task, though. We packed all of Saturday and all day Friday and Saturday of the next weekend. Living in the woods for sixteen days required a lot of preparation, materials, food, equipment, and knowledge. Along with some general wilderness safety teaching, we also received basic survival instructions and general first aid instructions.

The equipment required for each person, which was all packed into a backpack, was a collapsible sleeping bag, a blow-up ground mat, a tiny pillow, two sets of thermal underwear, socks, gloves, glove liners one set of ski pants and hoodie, one set of rain gear, one puffy heavy coat, one snow hat, sunglasses, compass, head lamp, water bottle, iodine tablets, ski boots, and cross-country skis.

In order to store the rest of the equipment, every other person was required to pull a five-foot-long pack attached to a sled. Two six-foot metal tubes extended from the sled and attached to a waist belt. Each pack held a tent, a mini gas stove, gas tanks, utensils, bowls, food, a snow shovel, and back-up equipment.

For food, we used a dehydrating machine to make homemade beef jerky and dried fruits. In gallon-sized bags each person packed cheese cubes, trail mix, Snickers bars, packets of soup, and hot chocolate. For community food, we packed tons of pasta, oat cereal, powdered milk, hot sauce, and salt seasoning. There was no meat source.

The week and a half had finally passed, the equipment was packed, and the next morning we were heading out. It was Sunday night and time for lights out. Sleeping was difficult, but I eventually let my thoughts slip into unconsciousness. Before I knew it, the night tech was shining his flashlight and instructing me to wake up. Since we were leaving early that morning, we were required to wake before the normal time.

The night tech's flashlight startled me, but I had no problem hopping straight out of bed. Finally, finally, the day of the Trip! I had only been at the facility four and a half weeks, but it felt like years. The Trip meant I was on the verge of completing the program, and I could not wait to return home. Slipping into the thermal underwear (that I would only change once over the next sixteen days), my thoughts flooded with excitement. Over the thermals were the thin ski pants and hoodie. It was not much clothing, but once we started skiing that's all we would need. Thermal gloves were next, along with a goofy-looking snow hat that tied under my chin or velcroed up around the top. A pair of sunglasses and a compass hung from my neck. Warm fuzzy boots were that last thing to put on. Since my feet were too big for the ski boots, I got to wear special sheep's wool, super-comfy boots. Everyone else had to wear rock hard, plastic ski boots. For the first time, I felt blessed to be so tall. Horror stories of the extremely uncomfortable boots had been floating around the Dub forever, and here I was walking around in the Rolls Royce of ski boots. Sweet!

Despite only being awake for a few minutes, I felt energized and alert. Throwing open the cabin door, the crisp, cold mountain air cleared my thoughts. I stomped across the porch and admired the dim sunlight just peeking over the mountain ranges. With the excitement of the Trip, my mind flooded with endorphins and I smiled at the beautiful mountain sunrise. What a special day! Off to my left, I noticed Germ stomping though the snow in his matching green suit. He smiled, waved, and started chanting, "We're going to the woods, we're going to the woods, we're going to the woods."

Normally, I would just laugh at someone singing like a moron, but I was so excited, I had to join in. Together, Germ and I marched through the snow to get to the dining hall. Smells of French toast and cinnamon sweetness filled the air. Germ and I were the first ones in the building, but no more than two minutes later came Chris, Bran, Thomas, Ken, and David, all wearing the same matching green suit, goofy hat, and necklace combination of sunglasses and compass. Smiles were running across everyone's faces, and Germ restarted the chant. Everyone joined in and we all sounded like fools chanting, "We're going to the woods."

Fools or not, though, to see excitement, peer bonding, happiness, and willingness to conquer challenges ahead felt like a godsend. The transformation was absolutely incredible. Anyone who had seen us when we first arrived would have never thought these kids would be acting like this only four and a half weeks later. Even to my own amazement, my attitude was completely different. The Dub had done wonderful things in all of us and we hadn't even gone to the woods yet.

Moments later, Wilder Andy and Counselor Bill came strolling in, decked out in their ski clothing, except they didn't have the sweet matching green ones we had. Andy was wearing all black material and Bill had blue pants and a white top. But when they moved their clothes made the same noise as ours, like garbage bags crinkled together.

We all took our hats and gloves off and snatched one of the faded turquoise plastic trays. Lining up and waiting for the counselors to get their food, Germ started the chant again. Counselor Bill looked at us in disbelief and slight disgust. He probably wasn't too thrilled about going to the woods for sixteen days, but that couldn't ruin our mood. We were pumped!

Breakfast only took about twenty minutes. Sounding like a band of marching trash bags, we filed out the door and over to the equipment shed. The two worn down, gray Suburbans were already cranked and spilling exhaust from the rear tailpipes. Appearing from behind one of the trucks, Carsten clapped, smiling, and said, "Woods, baby! This is it! The Trip!" This sparked up the chant and we started bouncing around like a bunch of jumping beans, flailing our arms in all directions. Carsten just laughed and wished us good luck, disappearing into the dining hall.

Bill and Andy opened the double doors in the back of the Suburbans and instructed, "Fill it up." Without question, we threw in the gear and piled in the back seats. The doors slammed shut and off we went bouncing down the snow-covered path.

The Trip

Including a halfway break, the ride to YellowStone National Park took three hours. It felt like three minutes. The Suburbans were stopping. We were on the side of a major highway and on top of a mountain. I jumped out and had it not been for the Suburbans to hold on to, the wind would have blown me over. It was crazy how strong the winds were blowing. Our green suits were about to blow off our bodies. I couldn't even hear what anyone was saying unless they screamed at the top of their lungs.

Across the highway was a drop-off, farther than you could see. That's why the winds were so strong. We were on top of the mountain with nothing to block the wind. On the opposite side was a snow field that stretched for several hundred yards, stopping at the tree line. The woods!

All of the sudden I heard Andy screaming, "Get moving!" My heart jumped. I raced to throw on the sixty-pound pack, strap on the sled, and jump into the skis. The first one ready, I stabbed the poles deep in the snow, leaned over, and thrust all my weight forward. Slowly, both skis started gliding on top of the snow. Lunging my right ski forward I continued to slide, but quickly pulled it back and lunged my left ski forward. It created a fluent motion. Right. Left. Right. Left. I was moving.

Halfway through the field, I looked back and noticed Germ creeping up. He didn't have a sled and was able to move faster, but the idea of pulling an eighty-pound sled had all of us worried. He was first to yell out, "Chad, how's the sled?" Looking back to direct my voice through the wind, I yelled, "It's fine." After that, I focused all attention forward to keep moving.

Moments later I passed through the tree line. It was like day and night, going from a tornado to absolute stillness. I continued skiing until I heard Andy yell, "STOP!" I tried, but the skis kept gliding. There were no brakes and the extra weight kept me moving. I didn't know what to do. I just kept sliding.

Finally the skis slowed enough to control the speed. I came to a standstill and waited for everyone to catch up. Germ came sliding up, winded, but smiling. He started chanting, "Yeah, we're in the woods, we're in the woods." Out of breath, I returned the smile and started chanting "What What, What What... We're in the woods... We're in the woods, yeah baby!"

All of a sudden Thomas slid toward us with a look of fear streaked across his face. He couldn't stop. He tried everything but nothing worked. Germ knew it. Helpless, Germ tried to lift the skis to move from the path of collision. It was too late. SLAM! Poles went flying, arms flailed, skis flung and they both bit the snow.

The heavy packs were awkward. It was hard enough to keep your own balance without having someone run into you. Germ stood no chance. Watching them try to stand was even better. Chunks of snow fell from all body parts, their arms flailed and their legs wobbled, much like a newborn fawn. Reluctantly they both took off the packs and used each other to get to their feet. Despite the struggle, they were both smiling.

The group came together and we started back up. The path was so still and so quiet as it carved crookedly through the dense snow-covered woods. It was about twenty feet wide. Without another soul in sight all we could hear were the noises of the skis gliding, the ski pants ruffling, and the metal poles clicking.

The path was nice and flat, but up ahead was a drop-off. Still new and wobbly on the skis, anxiety swarmed my body. I could only imagine myself face-planting the second I crossed the edge. Looking down, I focused all my attention on the terrain. The skis went sliding over the edge. It all seemed fine, until the sled crossed the edge. I went flying out of control. It was too quick! I tried to resist, tried not to fall, but the pack shifted in all directions.

To my surprise I passed safely over flat ground. Or so I thought. The force of the sled caught up and I went flying forward. My body buckled and my eyes caught sight of the ground. FACEPLANT! The hard snow scraped against my face. The cold felt like flames of fire.

With my face buried, I tried to pull up. The pack didn't allow it. I couldn't move. The snow was burning. Finally I twisted from the hips and flung the weight to the side. Lying twisted with the skis still attached and the poles stuck under my stomach, I tried to get up. I couldn't. I tried again. I couldn't. Eventually giving up, I unbuckled the sled, the pack, and took everything off. It was frustrating, but it was the only way.

With the group still moving, I hurried to brush off the snow, strap in, and catch up. Skiing was not tiring yet and for the most part it was fun. That didn't last long. For the next five hours we skied and skied and skied, only stopping twice for a quick water break. The sun was out, and even though it was freezing, my body was sweating. Skiing was a full-body workout. Pulling an eighty-pound sled along with a sixty-pound backpack was exhausting.

We skied five miles before finally gliding out of the woods into a wide open snow field. Off to the right, I noticed a small cluster of giant trees. Andy was in the lead and we followed, skiing toward the cluster. Only ten minutes later Andy stopped. Red-faced and winded, he looked over with a smile and said, "This is it."

"Yes! Finally!" I immediately unbuckled the straps and dropped the weight. "Wow! Oh wow, that feels nice!" Not having the straps digging into my skin felt incredible.

Moments later, Chris, Germ, Thomas, and Bran pulled up, carrying the same winded, red-faced, expression. Smiles ran across their faces as they dropped their packs. Day one of skiing was over. We were officially in the woods!

After only a few minutes of resting, Andy looked up at the setting sun. "All right, set it up. Put on your puffy jackets and cotton socks." He pointed at Thomas, Germ, and me saying, "You guys set up the tents."

He pointed at Ken and David, "You guys get out the cooking gear and food." Then his finger shifted to Chris and Bran and said, "You guys each grab a shovel and come with me."

We immediately went to work. Pitching the three tents took an hour. By the time we finished, the sun had set. To help see, I pulled on an elastic band with a light attached. Then I blew up the air mat, laid out the sleeping bag, and opened the tiny pillow.

Once it was set, I was curious to see what Chris and Bran were up to, so I stomped through the deep virgin snow. With the headlamp on, the puffy hoodie pulled over, and my steaming breath clouding in the lamp's rays, I felt like an astronaut on a strange planet.

By the time I reached them, my lungs were heavy and I was surprised to see them four feet deep, shoveling massive loads of snow over their shoulder. Confused by the sight I asked, "What are y'all doing?" Red-cheeked and winded, they didn't respond. They kept shoveling. I stood watching. Andy came up and nudged my arm. "What do you think?"

Still confused, I asked, "What is it?"

With a goofy grin he responded, "The kitchen, man."

"Ohhh yeah, I remember. It's weird."

He laughed and agreed.

Chris and Bran dug four feet deep and fifteen feet in diameter to create a sunken circle. Around the inside edge and half way up, they carved a flat surface to sit on. Near me, they carved two large steps and I stepped in, plopping down on the cold, snow seat. Moments later Ken and David reappeared, out of breath, each carrying two steel pots filled with water. After setting the pans down, spilling some water, they collapsed next to me.

Andy entered the kitchen, dropped a cylinder gas tank in my lap, and instructed, "Start pumping." A quarter-sized circle extended from the bottom that I pulled out and pushed in one thousand times before there was enough pressure to light. The gas tank sat in a small metal stand beneath a six-inch stove.

Finally, Andy had two stoves burning with pots full of water coming to a boil. The first portion of the meal was a powdered soup, either tomato or chicken noodle. Next came macaroni and cheese with Tabasco or salt for flavoring. I ate as many bowls as possible without leaving a single crumb. Since it was inevitable that wild animals would smell our camp, we had to be extra careful to not leave any cooked food behind. Without trash cans the only place to dispose of the macaroni was our stomachs. I felt like a balloon full of macaroni noodles about to pop. After dinner we packed the uncooked food in nylon tent bags and strung them from the trees.

Ken and David stomped back to the stream to clean the pots while the rest of us remained in the kitchen. It was time for the recovery meeting. That was the last thing any of us wanted to do, but we needed it. The meetings helped. However, our bellies were so full and our bodies were so tired that an hour felt like forever. The environment didn't help. It was dark and the cold air was unbearable. No matter how much clothing we wore, the cold snuck its way in. Our fingers were numb. The only way to keep them from falling off was to constantly flex and release them throughout the entire meeting.

The topic of the meeting was chosen by whoever chaired the meeting. Topics varied from night to night. A few common themes were "accepting we have a problem," "character flaws," or "starting a better life." Whether we admitted it or not, the meetings were crucial. They were the glue holding everything together. It was a time to express how we really felt. Since every day brought a new challenge or a new thought that could jeopardize the whole process of rehabilitation, it was crucial for us to get out of our own heads by verbalizing our feelings. Verbalizing brings irrational thoughts into a clear perspective, and that's what addiction is: a tricky little mind game. The mind creates all types of reasons to drink or use drugs. If you don't get those reasons or excuses out, they will turn into actions.

After the meeting we retired to bed. The tents barely held everyone, but in zero-degree weather body heat was crucial. Before going to sleep we took off the heavy cotton socks, the thin thermal socks, and the lining of the boots and stuffed them deep in the sleeping bag. Everything was wet, but throughout the night our body heat would dry it all out. To prevent skin rot, we kicked our feet vigorously like a bicycle in midair for two minutes. Once dry, I slipped on the other pair of heavy cotton socks, took off the ski suit, pulled on a cotton beanie, and snuggled deep into the sleeping bag. It seemed odd to be sleeping in only a thin layer of long underwear, but Andy insisted we would be fine. On the edge of the tent, pressed between Ken and the sloping wall, I pulled the cotton beanie over my eyes and zipped the sleeping bag over my face. With only a small hole to breathe from, I felt warm enough to sleep. I quickly dozed off.

I made a terrible mistake. I didn't go pee before bed. After waking in the middle of the night I tried to hold it. It was useless. Andy forced us to drink a full bottle of water an hour before bed to help prevent dehydration. Not wanting to wake anyone, I slowly zipped open the sleeping bag and sat up. My head bumped the ceiling and bits of ice rained down. *Aaaaa! What on earth! What is this! So cold! So cold!* The ice caused both Ken and Andy to stir. Moisture from our breath collected along the walls of the tent and froze. It created a thin layer of ice ready to fall with only the smallest movement. *How awful!* The last thing we needed was to get wet in the middle of the night.

After the ice storm, the process only got worse.   Slowly shimmying over to the door, I unzipped it, causing more ice to rain. Immediately, chilling wind rushed in. I sat on the edge trying to find my boots. The night before Andy had shoveled a two-foot-deep by three-foot-wide hole in front of the tent door to create a spot to sit and take off the boots. Trying to speed the process, I frantically searched through the pile of boots. Once I found them I had more problems. Throughout the night, the boots had collapsed and, frozen with ice. The strings were impossible to untie. There was simply no way of just slipping on the boots.

My fingers went numb from knocking off the ice, straightening the leather and forcing my feet in. Finally, I stomped through the snow and started to pee. The pee kept coming and coming and coming. *Come on. Come on. I'm freezing! This is terrible!* I was shaking and the frozen boots weren't helping. Standing in zero-degree temperatures with only thin underwear on, I needed the process to be as short as possible. It wasn't. Hours had passed before I finally stomped back to the tent, kicked off the boots, and nestled deep into the sleeping bag. What a pain!

Day Two

The next thing I knew, I heard Bill's voice outside the tent, "WAKE UP, BOYS, WAKE UP, BOYS, WAKE UP, BOYS." He clapped and yelled.

Shut up. Shut up! Shut up!

All I wanted to do was slap him in the face. Rubbing my sticky eyes, I started to poke out of the sleeping bag, but like a scared turtle I quickly pulled back in. *No way! Screw that! That's awful.* The cold air was too much and the sleeping bag was so warm. If I had a choice I would have slept all day, but Andy hit my arm. "Get up, no time to waste." *Maaan!* Reluctantly, I unzipped the bag and came face-to-face with the frigid air. Trying to slow the cold, I quickly pulled on the green suit and the puffy jacket. They didn't help. My teeth immediately started chattering. Barely awake and groggy, I deflated the mattress and tied it to the side of the pack. After rolling up the sleeping bag and pillow, I stuffed them deep in the pack, took off the heavy cotton socks, replaced them with the thin thermal socks, slipped on the boot linings, and shimmied to face the boots. They were still just as frozen. Somehow I managed to work my feet in and step out of the tent. The air was crisp, cold, and refreshing. The sun peaked over the mountains. Not even my grogginess could ruin this sight.

Out in the distance, I noticed Chris and Bran already journeying through the field to get to the water supply. *That sucks! Wait! Awww, noooo... My bottle is empty!* We had to drink two bottles before the day started, so I reluctantly joined the long march. Had I gotten out of bed a few minutes earlier, I could have asked them to fill my water bottle. I just missed my opportunity.

Ten minutes later and breathless, I reached the end. There was a twenty-foot drop where Chris and Bran were kneeling, struggling to fill the pots. I could have dropped the bottle to them, but I wanted to experience fetching raw mountain water. Jumping off the edge and sinking waist-deep in snow, I carefully worked my way down the hill. The stream was only an inch deep so filling the bottle was tricky. Once full I dropped in an iodine tablet, sat down and waited five minutes before chugging the entire bottle. *Oh wow! That's amazing.* The water was so fresh and so cold. Pieces of ice bumped against my warm lips. *This must be what people dream of when they drink their overpriced bottled water. You just can't beat raw, ice-cold mountain water straight from the source.*

After refilling the bottle, I stomped back to the frozen kitchen and plopped down. The hike was tiring. At least it warmed my body. Once everyone was in the kitchen, Chris passed around the bag of powdered milk and oat cereal. Since sanitation was not a luxury, we used the same bowl and same spoon for every meal.

Breakfast was pretty fun with Germ telling jokes and Bran doing impressions of Germ telling jokes. "Hey hey hey, guys, look," Bran opened his eyes real wide, opened his mouth, and danced around like a chicken. "Look at me, I'm a germ."

It was nice until Andy shot the mood down. "All right, we're behind schedule. Quit talking and finish up." That, of course, only provoked Germ, so he put on a goofy face and started mocking Andy. It actually made Andy laugh, but it was more of a nervous laugh.

After breakfast, as I was breaking down the tents I noticed yellowish hard spots where the tent had been. I couldn't figure it out, but Germ pointed and laughed. "Look at the prints of our bodies." *Aaah, now it made sense.* Throughout the night the snow melted from the body temperature and refroze in the morning. It looked like a big frozen pee spot.

About an hour later, the gear was packed. We were ready to hit the trail. The March sun was shining without a cloud in sight, and we circled for the daily reading. The overall process from wake to departure took about two hours. Andy was disgruntled. It was weird to seem him grouchy. He was always so happy and so goofy, but apparently he had a thing for keeping a schedule. We couldn't have cared less. He was pissed. He wanted us to be out of there in an hour and a half. *Whatever, dude.* The backpacks came on, Germ took the sled. Off we went, sliding, gliding, and pushing our way through the snow.

Not having the sled helped limit my wipeouts. However, for the group, it didn't matter. The terrain was hilly and on a down slope, at least one person always wiped out. It slowed the journey, aggravating those who survived. Someone always muttered under their breath, "Really, goshhh. Come on, let's go." Sooner or later, though, that person would eat snow. There was just no escaping it.

The temperature was warm, somewhere in the forties. The sweat was dripping. At least it wasn't raining, or snowing, or windy. I felt blessed. "Thank you God for this good weather." Germ and Bran gave an Amen.

Halfway through the journey we stopped for lunch. Trail mix was all we had, but it helped our energy levels. Besides, not wearing the packs was glorious. It wasn't so much the weight of the pack, it was way the straps dug into the skin. No matter how the pack was positioned, the pain just never ceased. We just had to accept the pain and block it out. That's what this trip was about—accepting the pain and continuing with the journey. For the alcoholic or addict, emotional pain is a strong source for continued abuse. The Trip was attempting to teach us that life is full of struggles and pain. All we wanted to do was escape through drugs and alcohol. That's not life.

We were learning to face the struggles and persevere in the correct manner.

Four hours into the journey, we started making our way up a narrow, twisty path. It felt like we climbed for days. The sweat was dripping, our faces were flushed, and our breath was almost gone. "Push! Push! Push!" Germ was in the back giving support. "Come on, guys, almost there! Push, we got this."

Finally we reached the peak. It wasn't as glorious as I imagined. A downhill that looked like the back of Satan himself stared us straight in the eyes. I took in a deep breath as my skis crossed the peak. Down I went, twisting and turning, almost crashing every twenty feet. The speed was too intense. The adrenaline rushed through my veins. Before long, I came flying around the last curve. The path straightened to a flat surface. Andy was at a standstill and I tried to slow down. The speed was raging. I went flying by Andy, almost knocking him over again. I didn't wipe out though. I couldn't believe it! Thirty yards later I finally slowed enough to stop and worked my way back. With his goofy grin, he said, "This is it, campsite number two."

"Yes, thank goodness." I almost melted with relief as I dropped the pack.

All of a sudden, I heard someone yelling from around the corner. Thomas! Not again! With the sled attached, he looked like an out-of-control rocket ship headed right for us. He tried to control the speed. The weight was too much. He flew by and zoomed up the side of the embankment, face-planting deep in the snow. Skis, poles, and equipment went flying. Andy and I cried with laughter. Moments passed before he finally sat up. With a face full of snow, he whined, "Not funny." *Yeah right, it's hilarious!* And I collapsed in the snow laughing and hooting.

Once everyone had either blown by or wiped out, we came together and immediately put on the warm clothes and separated into jobs. Andy assigned Germ and me to build the kitchen. I grabbed the shovel and started digging. It felt like I was digging a grave. After skiing all day, I might as well have been digging my own grave. Over an hour of shoveling passed before I collapsed on the snow seat. My skin was moist with sweat and the cold air made me feel like I was a Popsicle. Then I heard Andy out in the trees shout,

"WE'VE STRUCK OIL!" Not oil, just water—but it felt like gold. I loved the cold mountain water.

The night went the same way: soup, pasta, a recovery meeting. It couldn't have been any later than eight o'clock when we went to bed. The only thing we needed was the comfort of the warm sleeping bag.

Days Three, Four, Five, and Six

Cold, sweat, wind, work, cold, cold, cold, and more cold dampened everyone's mood. There were no more chants of excitement, no more smiles of fun, no more jolly singing, just hard work. The constant freezing temperatures ruined everyone's happy images of the woods.

Only when we were skiing were we warm. Then we would get too warm and the wind would freeze the sweat. There was never a time we felt comfortable. Not to mention we had developed a life of ease by escaping through drugs and alcohol. Here we were experiencing the most amount of bone-chilling hard work any of us had experienced. Realistically, it was just what we needed. The woods were teaching us to push our pain threshold. Maybe if it hadn't been so cold it might have been bearable, but there was no escaping the cold. After skiing all day, there was nothing left to stay warm. Even when we were constantly moving when setting up camp, the frozen air was too much. By now setting up camp was annoying. We resented stomping around in powdered snow, setting up tents, fetching water from who-knows-where, cooking dinner, and sitting through a full hour of a recovery meeting. The woods were past being old, and we were only a third of the way in.

Days Seven and Eight

After half a day of skiing on day seven, we reached an unusual camp site. It had a small log cabin, an outhouse, and an actual spigot for water. The site seemed odd, but a water supply meant we didn't have to dig for water. It was the only thing that gave us a glimmer of cheer. Fetching water was tiring.

Finally I figured out the log cabin was a park ranger post. I tried to open the wooden door. Nothing, it was locked so I collapsed on the worn wooden porch. We needed the rest. After rubbing my eyes,

I looked over at the outhouse. It had giant claw marks streaked all the way down the door. Bear marks! There was no doubt. Shreds of brown paint were lying near the bottom. It looked like a ranger had been trapped in the house by the bear. Maybe I should have been more concerned about the massive claw marks, but after six days of being in the woods, nothing concerned me.

Even the beauty of surrounding snow-covered mountains, frosted green trees, and breathtaking sunsets were not enough to warm my soul. All I wanted was a shower, fresh clothes, electricity and toilet paper. In the woods, there was no toilet paper, only sticks, leaves, and snow. My rear always felt like...

The sun was beaming. I became frustrated as I searched for a comfortable position on the hard wooden planks. In front of the porch was a massive field that gently sloped for days before it stopped at a tree line—the campsite. For the time being, Andy allowed us to relax. I quickly slipped away.

For the first time, I woke without someone forcing me to. The sun was still beaming and I rubbed my sticky, cloudy eyes. We were not allowed to bring contact supplies, so if I wanted to see anything, I had to sleep in them. It's the worst, but I had no choice. When I woke up with my contacts still in, it took at least ten minutes of squinting, blinking, and rubbing before my vision cleared. There is nothing easy about the woods.

Twenty minutes later, everyone was fully awake. Feeling refreshed, we decided to set up camp. It took the usual hour. Once we were done there was still plenty of daylight. Andy pointed to a path in the trees, opening to the base of a hill and said, "Hey guys, if you want, go criss-cross up that hill and do a little downhill skiing." It actually sounded fun, but downhill skiing is difficult in cross-country skies. Without the heel attached, there is less control of the ski. Of course we wiped out, but it was fun. Smiles and cheer floated among us as we went flying back and forth.

After my third descent, I started working my way back up when I noticed Thomas climbing to a part where no one had ever been. *Oh no! What is he doing?! Ha ha, this is going to be great!* Once he reached the highest point, he bombed straight down, not even pretending to slow his speed. Halfway down he realized the speed was too much. He tried to slow down, but it was too late. The skis wobbled out of control, and when he caught an edge, his body went flying through the air. Seconds passed before he hit the snow and tumbled over and over and over. Skis, poles, and gloves went flying and by the time the cloud came to a rest, he sat up dazed and delirious. It was the worst wipeout we had ever seen. Both skis were sticking straight out of the snow. The poles were bent, resting in the snow. Gloves were nowhere to be seen and his sunglasses were crooked. It was so funny that I took a picture with the disposable camera we had been given to capture the trip.

The next morning, day eight, Andy said, "Well boys, leave camp set. Today we're climbing a mountain." *Hmm... this might be bad, but it could be better than heavy packs digging into my shoulders.* The skin on my shoulders was worn raw.

Immediately after breakfast we marched with only our ski poles to meet a giant river. The river was wider than four lanes of traffic. Pieces of ice were floating past us. Giant brown rocks jutted from the water. Large rapids rushed the ice down the river. *How are we ever going to cross this! This is nuts!* Andy didn't hesitate and jumped from rock to rock like a monkey. *What?! Wow! Jeez. If I fall it's all over.* The rocks looked slippery, the ice looked like death, and the water made me cringe. It didn't matter. Everyone had to cross. I let out a sigh before slowly extending one foot. Holding my breath I transferred all weight on to the rock. It slid. My heart skipped. I held on. I stuck the poles in the gravel river bed and balanced myself. The force of the water pushed against them. No time to waste. Repeating the process, I hopped from one slippery rock to the next. Not too fast though. *If I slip, I'm done.* My last step landed safely in the snow on the opposite side. *Whew!* I made it. My nerves settled. I watched the others squirm. Bill was having the hardest time. His face was full of fear. A fatal mistake. You must have confidence when doing these things. His boot slid off the rock, splashing into the frozen water. Game over! As quick as he slipped, he hopped back onto the rocks and managed to get to the embankment. Andy knew he was done though. The only thing we could think to do was let Bill wear Andy's super comfortable cotton boots and hope the hike dried his feet.

Once he was ready we hiked a few football field lengths around the base of the mountain. This is where we began the climb. The first half was bearable, only taking an hour to climb, but the last half was too steep to walk. We had to crawl. With every movement we sank two feet into the snow. It was so hard. Had we not been in good shape from skiing for seven days, there is no way all of us would have made it up that mountain.

The last section of the climb was the steepest. There was no snow, just different sized rocks. The terrain was so steep that if we happened to slip, we would tumble for who knows how long. It spiked fear in everyone's veins. No one spoke, we just climbed. More than a couple times, one of my feet slipped. My heart jumped. Somehow I managed to put enough weight on the other foot to stop myself from tumbling down the mountain.

The climb took all day, but the view at the top was worth it. In every direction were the peaks of jagged, snow covered mountains, frosted trees and an occasional cloud. I took out my disposable camera, snapped a few shots, and soaked in the surge of endorphins released from the climb. It was spiritual.

Because the climb had taken all day, the sun was on the verge of setting. After thirty minutes of gazing, we frolicked down the entire mountain in less than two hours. We passed back into camp a few moments before the sun went to sleep.

Days Nine and Ten – The Cabin!

After a full twenty-four hours of not wearing the pack, my upper body felt refreshed. As we skied to camp, a new type of soreness in my legs burned with each push or pull. It was from the climb. No matter what, we could never get away from agonizing soreness pulsing in some portion of our bodies. There was no relief. *Block it out and keep moving.* Relief only came when we slept. It was never enough. We desperately needed a break and thank goodness day ten promised that—we just had to get through day nine.

Our bodies were worn out, and wiping out was becoming even more frequent. We were crashing left and right. It was killing the mood. There is nothing worse than crashing. The moment right before you hit the ground is beyond nerve-wracking. You knew you were going down and all you could do was brace for the impact. It hurt every time, some falls worse than others. Depending on the fall, I usually ended up with a bruise, a face full of snow, pants full of snow, a shirt full of snow, a twisted limb, and always a higher level of frustration.

The physical pain was somewhat tolerable, but the frustration was like a disease. After a wipeout the process of getting up was so annoying. As you braced for impact, you could only pray you would be able to pop up and keep skiing. Nine times out of ten no one was that fortunate. Instead, one or both skis would blow off and a pole or two would be launched from a failed attempt at stabilizing. Then you would fall backward, smacking your head against the snow or face plant forward. Either way, the pack prevented us from moving. If someone was pulling a sled, the impact would send the strap up around his chest with the metal poles twisting like a candy cane. No matter what, the pack and the sled had to be taken off. Sometimes the wipeout was so bad everyone stopped to eat while belongings were hunted down. At least for the people not involved, it gave comic relief, but overall a wipeout increased time on the trail. The last thing anyone wanted was more time on the trail.

Day ten and after only a few hours of skiing, glimpses of colors were in sight. Through the staggered trees I saw reds, blacks, and unnatural greens. It took a few moments, but once I got closer I couldn't believe my eyes. THE CABIN!! Finally! Warmth! And like kids with ice cream, we shouted with pure joy.

Minutes later, we pulled up, dropped the packs, and kissed the wooden boards of the porch. Civilization! It was an absolute godsend. Behind us, only forty feet away, was a wide flowing stream. My throat was dry, so I took a moment to drink while Andy searched for the key. This called for a celebration. I was going to change my clothes tonight. I had been holding out to truly appreciate the cabin—even though I had been ten days without a shower.

For the first time, I saw my reflection in the frosted windows. Staring back in the faded glass was a face I almost didn't recognize. The oil on my head had turned my hair black and matted like a homeless person. My facial hair was patchy. My skin looked like I rubbed greasy pepperonis all over it. *Jeez, who am I?*

Andy popped open the creaky wooden door and we stomped in with joy. Old wooden floors covered the ground and the smell of staleness filled the room. No one had been there in weeks. Sheets were draped over everything. Straight ahead were eight bunk beds, a dining table, and a kitchen. Off to the right were a set of stairs barricaded to prevent anyone from going up. Overall, the cabin looked the way a cabin should look. The color of stained wood, old scenic artworks scattered about, hanging animal heads, a stone fire place, a couple of bear skins, some random antique knickknacks, and a quilt hanging on the wall. We only gazed for a few seconds before Andy ordered, "Bring in the gear, start the fire, and fetch six buckets of water." He pointed at a stack of five-gallon white buckets. We went straight to work.

Near the fireplace was a green cord tied from one side of the cabin to the other. Using the clothes pins, we hung our clothes, sleeping bags, and tents. Since the snow got into everything, the gear was in desperate need of being dried out. The sleeping bags were moist from the nightly showers of falling ice, the packs were soaked from the numerous wipeouts and the clothes were damp with sweat.

After hanging the gear, Germ and I started the fire. A fire! We couldn't believe we had warmth. It felt like we crossed into heaven as we soaked up every ray of heat. My eyes glazed with comfort and I melted into the wooden floor. There was plenty of wood so throughout the night we could keep it going. Anytime someone had to pee, that person threw on a log.

For dinner we actually had a protein source, fried chicken, and even better, Andy baked a cake—a strawberry vanilla cake. I had never appreciated warmth, normal food and lights like that in my entire life. Drugs and alcohol? What's that? All I needed was warmth, food, and lighting. My thoughts had gone from drug abusing mode to survival mode—just what the Trip was meant to do.

After dinner we flopped onto the multicolored, seventies-era couches surrounding the fire place and waited nervously for the moment of truth: the moment when we were told what our futures held after completing the wilderness program. All I wanted was to go home, to go back to a normal life, and to not attend another program. Surely my parents would bring me home. Surely I wouldn't have to go somewhere else. *Please... Please... Please... Bring me home.*

Bill went down the line like he was handing out jail sentences. Maybe not as bad as jail sentences, but deep down everyone wanted to go home. That wasn't our decision. Our decisions got us a life of agony with drugs and alcohol. If we wanted any chance of surviving, we had to rely on what other people thought was best for us.

By this point, after everything we had been through, we were willing to accept whatever came our way. I mean, it can't get any worse than living in the snow. It may not have been what we wanted, but the program was teaching us to accept the things we cannot change. Crucial for our survival. In the past I never accepted the things that were best for me. I always fought for my way and if I didn't get it, well, I'd just go get high.

When Bill finally came to me, I felt absolutely certain my parents were going to bring me home. I just knew it. This was more than enough. I'm not a bad kid. Bill's mouth opened to tell my future: a three-month halfway house in Wayzata, Minnesota. My heart didn't sink and I didn't freak out, I just accepted my fate and trusted it was best for me.

I wasn't a crusted, stale person anymore and just demonstrated for the first time the ability to accept the things I cannot change— besides, Germ was going to the same place. Realistically, it could have been worse. The program could have been six months or even a year at one of the dreaded halfway houses. Germ grew up in Wayzata, Minnesota, and he said it would be great. Great? Did he really just say that? What happened to us? The Trip happened to us!

That night sleeping indoors was actually not easy. We had been so used to sleeping on the cold snow surface that the spring bunk bed mattress didn't feel normal. About every hour I woke up and threw a log on the fire or went to pee in the metal "thunder bucket." I never dreamed I would someday be peeing in a metal bucket. Then again, never did I imagine myself not showering for sixteen days. The smell of us combined was absolutely disgusting. It could have been used for gas in chemical warfare weapons.

Three Days of Isolation: Day One

The next morning marked the beginning of the hardest part of the Trip. Three days of isolation with only our clothes, a snow shovel, trail mix, water, a sleeping bag, and a blue tarp. No tent. One by one, Andy called us out of the house and took each person in a different direction. I was excited. At least we didn't have to ski, lug around the pack, pull the sled, and set up camp. We just had to stay within a fifty-yard by fifty-yard area for three days and three nights, all by ourselves. Andy skied out a boundary zone and said, "If you step out of the boundaries you will be forced to go on another Trip." Scared to death, I made sure to never even come within five feet of the boundary line. There was no reason to test the waters.

Since we weren't allowed to have a tent, we had to build some kind of shelter. A few days earlier, Andy demonstrated how to build an igloo. After piling up a mound of snow six-feet-tall by ten-feet-long, I packed the mound by slapping it all over with the back of the shovel. Once packed, I waited two hours for the sun to harden the unturned snow. After the mound hardened, I took about fifty, six-inch-long sticks and stuck them all over. The sticks signaled where to stop shoveling from the inside. The process of making a home started by carving out a tire-sized hole for the front door. Once it was big enough to crawl through, I shoveled and shoveled and shoveled the insides. Ice rained down with every thrust of the shovel. The freezing bits landed on the back of my neck. It made me cringe.

The second I hit the butt end of a stick, I quit digging and moved to a different spot. The shoveling process took over an hour and after carving the ceiling, I was soaked with melted snow and sweat. Ready to take off the wet clothes, I threw open the blue tarp and laid out the sleeping bag.

The igloo was so large the small amount of light creeping in only allowed for minimal visibility. I purposely built the igloo large enough to stretch all the way out without being too close to the door. Also, I wanted to be able to pee in the corner. No matter how little water I drank, peeing in the middle of the night was still a regular occurrence. It was the worst. I would do anything to not have to crawl out in the frigid air to pee. OK, so peeing in the corner doesn't sound like the most pleasant thing, but after ten days of not showering and only changing clothes once, hygiene was the last thing on my mind.

Still wet, I took everything off and stuffed it all in the bottom of the sleeping bag. The only thing I wanted after the last ten days was to not ski, not work, and just go to sleep. Finally, some true rest and I passed out on the cold snow floor.

"Hey, Chad, get out here. Come on, get out here now."

Huh? What? Where am I? Confused and groggy, I opened my eyes and remembered I was in an igloo. The sun was almost gone as I crawled out. Despite the sticky contacts I could see Bill standing above me on skis and holding a pack. I watched him as he pulled out a metal canteen. He reached down and poured steaming hot water into my soup cup. After filling the cup, he screwed on the metal cap and pulled out a pack of cold water. With this he filled my bottle.

There was hardly any exchange of words before he awkwardly lifted his skis, turned around, and went gliding away. Wanting to stay warm, I crawled back into the igloo, stuck my legs in the sleeping bag and quickly drank the soup. Like a giant squirrel I chomped down some trail mix and burrowed back into my nest.

Three Days of Isolation: Day Two

I woke in the middle of night, peed in the corner, glanced outside at the falling snow and nestled deep into the sleeping bag. Compared to the tents, sleeping in the igloo felt like a blessing. Snow maintains thirty-two degrees, so the temperature inside the igloo was thirty-two degrees warmer than sleeping in the tents. Even better, the solid snow walls didn't collect moisture nor were there any annoying winds. It was actually comfortable and I slept soundly the rest of the night.

The next morning my eyes opened to sunlight beaming through the hole and the sound of Bill's voice echoing through the igloo. All I wanted to do was sleep. Bill was already back for another round of warm water and a refill for the water bottle. Reluctantly, I crawled out, took the water for the powdered soup and went back to sleep. Even after sleeping from the middle of the afternoon all the way though the night, my body was still pleading for more rest. It wasn't until late afternoon that I woke up.

The weather seemed nice, so like a bear coming from hibernation, I crawled out and looked up at the sun. It must have been between two and four. We were supposed to be working on our Phase Four packet, which is a twenty-page moral inventory. Each page asked one question that prompted us to write every substance-related wrongdoing we had afflicted upon someone else. *Yeah... Well... I'll do that later.* I had to burn the stored up energy created from sleeping for twenty-four hours. Snatching the awkward grey snow shovel, I started digging and digging and digging. I dug four feet down, hitting the frozen ground, and then dug in all directions. I created waist-deep channels, criss-crossing and weaving throughout the entire marked off area—but not too close to the boundaries! In some parts of the winding channels, I left small bridges to ski over. Even though I was sweating like a dog, I just kept digging and digging and digging. There was nothing else to do and it passed the time. That's all that mattered. The quicker the three days passed, the quicker I got to warmth, electricity, regular meals, and most importantly a hot, hot, hot shower.

Hours later, I ran through the channels, jumping over the different paths like a little kid. Eleven days in the woods, combined with a day and half by myself, and things like this were inevitable. I was getting a little loopy. I had to do something to take my mind off the reality of where I was.

My body finally tired enough to take a nap and without any problem I crashed until Bill's voice came echoing through the igloo. *Who else?* It was so annoying. I crawled out to see his expression full of amazement and disbelief at my freshly dug channels.   It looked a lot like the inside of an ant hill. Bill's expression was more than enough to realize how odd it really was. He didn't even say anything, just shook his head and laughed. After giving me the water he tried to ski away. He couldn't figure out how to exit the maze. I had strategically created only a few bridges to cross the channels. *Haha, gotch ya!* Bill backtracked, tried a new route and failed. Again, he backtracked, tried a new route and failed. I couldn't stop laughing. Hours seem to pass before he finally figured it out.

After that much entertainment, I was wide awake. It was almost dark and I was done with digging. Realizing there was nothing left to do, I unzipped the gallon-sized bag containing the phase four packet and pulled it out.

This was not going to be fun, but I knew I had to do it. I had to face every wrong thing I had done. It was the only way to clear my head and start down a new path. Thanks to the woods and the facility, I was ready for a new path.

Across the top of page one was written, "List all the people that you have directly hurt from drugs or alcohol or both." The rest of the page was blank and sadly, I had no issue covering every inch with black ink. There were another twenty pages and I wrote and wrote and wrote.

It was not easy to write down my wrongdoings. It pinched, pulled, and brought back intense levels of shame that I had not felt since Family Week. This time it was different. I was OK with facing the shame, because I remembered how good it felt to get everything out of my head.

Sleeping that night was a bit more difficult. The small area was getting to me, plus I had been sleeping way too much. Cabin fever was definitely setting in. I longed for the isolation period to be over. The only thing to do was sleep, but that wasn't happening. Instead, I stared at the snow ceiling and counted the protruding ends of the sticks. I never really knew what time it was, especially at night. It took hours of thinking and thinking and thinking before I finally fell asleep.

Three Days of Isolation: Day Three

The next morning I woke way too early. There was just no chance of sleeping the day away. Disappointed, I sat up and debated what to do. It's not that the three days were miserable. I mean, it was a great time to talk to God and really look at myself, but I could only do so much. Now it was just getting redundant. Sitting up in the sleeping bag, I choked down the same bag of trail mix and swigged some water before pacing around the small square. There was nothing else to do. I had completed the packet, I had dug channels though my entire area, we weren't allowed to climb trees, and I had skied the snow raw, so I just paced and paced and paced. Well, actually, I probably only paced for about ten minutes. Pacing was old too. I tried to go back to sleep. That went nowhere. I started memorizing the opening reading of the recovery meetings. It was as entertaining as staring at a blank wall. I gave up and just stared at the snow ceiling. My ears stayed perked for the sounds of skis. Twenty minutes later I heard Bill approaching. Excitement stormed through my body. I quickly crawled out, expecting him to say "You're done."

Nope. He poured the water and said he'd be back. *Nooooooo. No. No. No. Damn it! This sucks! More time! I am going crazy.* The frustration filled my veins. I couldn't believe it. Full of anger, I grabbed the shovel and starting crushing the walls of the channels. It helped. Better to dismantle the channels now anyways. I knew Bill would make me cover my tracks.

Only thirty minutes passed before I was back to doing nothing. Hoping I would maybe be tired enough to go to sleep, I snuggled in the sleeping bag. My wandering mind kept me awake. Time crawled by. I was so bored. *I hate being bored. It makes me want to get*

messed up. Maybe that's what this was about. Teaching us to deal
with boredom. I don't know. I just want to leave.

The sun had passed noon. Still no sign of Bill. I had given up on
anything to pass the time and just laid in my sleeping bag, listening
for approaching skis. Still nothing. More seconds, more minutes,
more hours passed... No Bill. I felt like a kid waiting for Christmas.

The sun was close to setting before I finally heard the clicking
and gliding of approaching skis. YES! I immediately poked my head
out. Bill exclaimed, "You're done! Break down the igloo and come
back to the cabin." WOOO HOOOO! I hadn't been this excited in
months. With no hesitation, I scrambled to pack the gear and crush
the igloo. Well, I tried to crush the igloo. Not even walking across
the top with over two hundred pounds of weight collapsed the thing.
It took ten strong jumps before I fell through the roof. Like a
chipmunk, I stuck my head out and pulled down the giant pieces. I
strapped on the skis, threw on the pack, and skied the victory path to
the cabin.

Excitement streamed through me. I noticed Germ, Thomas, and
Chris all approaching from different directions. Everyone threw up
their arms and shouted in happiness. We had done it! We had
completed three days of isolation and the end of the Trip was within
reach. That's what really mattered—getting back to the facility. With
the three days behind us, we could practically feel the warmth of a
bed and the trickling shower water.

That night we stayed in the cabin again to dry out the gear and
prepare for the last two days before the final push back to the
Suburbans. Even better, that night we had a warm meal that wasn't
trail mix. I was so done with trail mix.

Day Fourteen

Snow was falling as we departed from the cabin. During the
whole trip we had been lucky enough to not deal with falling snow.
Our luck just ran out. Didn't matter though—our spirits were high.

That didn't last long. Nothing exciting lasts long in the woods.
The cold ruins everything. As we skied, the snow collected on our
hats, shoulders, and packs. We looked like moving snowmen in the
swirling winds.

Skiing became nearly impossible. In fresh powder you don't glide on top of the snow. You sink and attempt to carve through it. It felt like there were thirty pound dumbbells on each ski. Even worse, twenty yards ahead was a path that seemed to touch heaven's pearly white gates. What a nightmare. At least I didn't have a sled. That didn't matter though. The powder was too much. I decided to do what I had done at every obstacle—suck it up and keep moving. Zone out. Think about anything besides the climb. But the powder was doubling the effort. I couldn't get the pain out of my head. The burning in my legs, the gasping for air, the freezing snow, the heavy pack... It all hurt. Every bit of it. It was breaking everyone. *Keep moving, keep moving.* We were strong. We could do it. *But it hurts. No, we can do it.*

Thomas was grunting and screaming, Chris was huffing and puffing, Germ was grinding his teeth. The only thing that gave us hope was the possibility of coming around a curve to find a flat surface. Only disappointment awaited. Surely we would reach a flat surface. Nope. We kept climbing and climbing and climbing and pushing and pushing and pushing. The snow kept falling and falling and falling.

Thomas was in the back pulling a sled. It weighed as much as he did. I looked back just in time to see him collapse into the snow. Through the heavy chunks of snow I saw Andy help him up and demand he keep moving. It lasted for a few minutes before he collapsed again. His face was bright red, his lungs were puffing, and his eyes rolled back in his head. It wrenched my heart and I knew he wasn't going another inch.

This had never happened before. Sure, there were moments when we felt we could not go on, but no one ever actually acted on it. Thomas's collapse demonstrated just how hard this climb was. Because I realized we needed to keep moving, I felt no choice other than to take Thomas's burden. It was the last thing I wanted to do. I was on the verge of collapsing myself. Another eighty pounds! I couldn't believe I was really thinking about taking his sled. *What? No way! Don't do it! But Thomas... Look at him.* He agonized in pain and exhaustion. *Do it! You have to.*

I skied back to where he was and took the straps. The look of complete relief mixed with the strongest gratitude made me swell up with pride. I was actually helping someone when I could barely help myself. Both Andy and Bill's faces instantly lit up with joy. They cared about us and to see me demonstrating selfless behavior was a true step toward recovery. That's all they really wanted to see—us making steps to recovery. For the first time in a long time, I voluntarily helped someone else. The Trip and facility were working!

The climb still did not end and the snow only came down harder. In the six inches of fresh powder our skis felt like a butter knife trying to cut a piece of cooked meat. Our bodies were shot, but we had to keep moving. Besides, the quicker we got up the mountain, the sooner we got to camp.

Another hour of climbing passed. Finally, Andy skied up next to me, took the lead, and peeled off the trail. We slid down a small path to the camp site. *No way!* We had done it! We conquered the mountain! The feeling didn't last. Our bodies were frail with fatigue. The whipping winds were blowing snow all over us.

The camp site was in the trees. We were on the edge of a mountain and the winds were relentless. There was a sharp drop-off only feet from the tents. Andy demanded we set up. It was the last thing anyone wanted to do, but it had to get done so we went to work. The wind whipped our faces raw and the fresh powder covered us from head to toe. We were in a true blizzard. We were also on top of a mountain where the wind blows no matter what. Had it not been for the hope of getting into a tent, we may have just given up and collapsed into an eternal dirt nap. But we didn't, and despite the tent material being ripped from our hands, we set it up! We defeated the day!

Before dinner, we had enough time to burrow into the sleeping bags to take a break. None of us had anything left. We had to get warmth and rest before going back out there. Even in the tents, the whipping winds affected us. The strong winds were blowing, pushing, pulling, and lifting the tent material in all directions. The parachute material slapped the sides of the sleeping bags.

Dinner was completed without a word spoken. It took too much energy to talk. The only thing to do was huddle together. Instead of conducting the recovery meeting in the snow kitchen, we took shelter in the tents. The slapping tent material was obnoxious, but at least we weren't covered in snow. Once the meeting was over, we went straight to sleep. Our bodies had given up.

Day Fifteen

Whooosh. Whoooosh. Whooooosh. The winds remained and today I was in charge of fetching the water. The thought of getting out of the tent sounded absolutely dreadful. The tent material was slapping even harder. Andy was yelling over the winds, "Chaaaad, get the water!" No, no, no. All I wanted was sleep, warmth, a shower, electricity, and shelter, but noooo, I had to step into a mountainside blizzard and fetch pots of water from a tiny stream a few hundred yards down the mountain. I was so over this. Fourteen days of cold and I was at my breaking point. My mental and physical strength were shot. Somehow I forced myself out of the tent, into the whipping winds, and down the side of the mountain. I couldn't walk in four feet of snow. I hopped, jumped, and kicked my way through. It's not all that bad going down, but I couldn't imagine how I was going to get up with two steel pots full of water. Just getting down the incline took over ten minutes.

I filled the pots and reluctantly faced the challenge. The best way was to follow my same tracks. It was still too much. I had to take three different breaks to catch my breath. Holding steel pots full of water with no support was nearly impossible. Half the water was gone when I finally reached the site.

Today was supposed to be another mountain climb. Surely Andy was not going to make us climb in the deadly winds and swirling snow. I prayed that we wouldn't have to go out there. Chances were we would.

During breakfast, we huddled close together again. Germ asked Andy what we were all thinking. "Are you really going to make us climb a mountain today in these conditions?" Our faces held expressions of hope and anxiety as we waited for Andy to respond. He remained quiet, just looking at his bowl of cereal, then took a bite. My mind raced with anxiety. *Please say no. Please say no. Please say no. Well hell, say something.* He never did, he just stayed quiet and no one else raised the question. The last thing we wanted to do was irritate him to a point of taking us on the climb just out of spite, so we sat in silence eating our cold cereal.

Breakfast was complete. Still no answer from Andy. Instead he instructed, "Go back to the tent and wait." It was not a "no" or a "yes," but it gave us a glimmer of hope. Our bodies were toast, our motivation was depleted, our mental strength didn't exist and here we were about to face the worst day yet. I wasn't sure if we could make it. The climb from the day before had destroyed us. There was nothing left.

Thirty minutes passed and still no answer. My ears perked to the sound of Andy unzipping the tent and stomping around before going back in the tent, never saying a word. All we could do was lie in our sleeping bags, holding our breath for a favored response.

My mind raced with hope, anxiety, and anticipation. Finally Andy yelled out, "We're not going. Stay in the tents, get some rest, and conduct a recovery meeting." *Sweet! No way! Yipeeee!* It was a true gift from God. We erupted with shouts of glee. The Trip practically felt over and tomorrow we were going home. What a blessing.

The rest of the day we stayed in the tent, only coming out for dinner.

Day Sixteen: Homeward Bound!

The next morning, I awoke before Andy gave the usual morning wake up call. The whipping winds made it hard to sleep. That didn't matter now. We were going home!

I continued to lie in my sleeping bag, staring at the pulsing tent material. It wasn't long before Andy gave the wake up call. We practically jumped out of the sleeping bags and started packing. We would usually drag out the morning process, not wanting to face the cold. Today was different. We could not wait to get going. The quicker we got up, the quicker we packed, and the quicker we got on the path. Warm cloth seats and blowing heated vents were waiting. It sounded like a dream. I could not believe today was the day. Finally! It felt like we had been in the woods for months.

Packing camp was not easy. The blowing snow and deadly winds made everything twice as hard. We couldn't grip the tent. We couldn't roll the tarps. We couldn't close the zippers. We could barely think.

It took two hours of struggling before we were packed. Finally! The layer of fresh powder was well over a foot deep. We didn't care. Nothing could ruin this mood.

We did get out of the wind, but after only thirty minutes of skiing the deep snow had taken its toll. Even going down the hills was a struggle. The powder changed everything. We were pushing to get down the hill. *What? No! Are we going uphill or downhill?* It all felt the same. Every twenty minutes we rotated the lead guy. Carving the path as point man was exahusting. Had it not been the last day of the Trip, several of us would have flat-out refused to go on. Exhaustion was written all over us. Our faces were purple, our lungs were heavy, our arms and legs were nearly numb with pain, and the giant snowflakes were melting on our cheeks. We pushed and pushed, grunting and shouting and grunting and shouting. The motivation was disappearing. We needed something. Germ was in the back and started singing a country song. Singing took our minds off the grind and our speed picked up. It didn't last. We went back to a snail's pace.

It felt like we were never going to reach the end. Seconds passed. Minutes passed. Hours passed and still no sign of the Suburbans. It was another full day of skiing and my mind wallowed in pain after every turn—I just saw more and more woods. I tried to be hopeful, picturing the moment when my eyes would finally see those beautiful, beautiful, beautiful Suburbans.

Eventually I blocked out even thinking about the Suburbans and just focused on the skis in front. The day had started with so much hope. The hope was all gone. The setting sun was crushing my dreams. *Are we gonna make it today? Oh no, are we gonna have to set up camp again? No, please no. But it's almost dark. Come onnnn. Come on. Come on. When is this journey ever going to end?* My mind obsessed and occasionally I looked up in hopes of seeing something. This just left me even more depressed. It never ended.

WHAT! What's that!? In front, Germ was yelling something. My eyes darted up. There they were! I could see them! Chills shot through my body. My speed tripled. We had done it! The end was visible! No way! No way! No way! As I raced forward, tears of joy swelled in my eyes. I couldn't believe it. Standing next to the Suburbans were two of the maintenance guys, waiting with smiles. I almost fell into their arms with relief. Immediately, I ripped off the packs, dropped the poles, and hopped out of the skis. It was over!

We had done it! We had gone where few have gone. We conquered the sixteen-day Trip!

Nine More Days

After dropping the gear, I watched as everyone came trickling in. Smiles were everywhere. Relief was everywhere. Peace was everywhere. We had just survived an all-out battle. How? I don't know. That didn't matter now, it was over. Never again!

We stomped around giving high fives. Not hugs though. We smelled worse than the bottom of a dumpster. Who knows what bacteria the other guy had crawling on him! Even the maintenance guys gagged as they helped load the gear. We just laughed.

Pulling on the steel handle, I threw open the door and jumped into Suburban heaven. A cloth seat and blowing heated vents! There was nothing else I needed. *Are we really in the Suburbans? No way! No more snow. No more cold. This must be how winning the lottery feels!*

The gear was loaded, everyone was in, and the maintenance guys zoomed off. Our smell was so strong that the first thing the driver did was roll down the window. Without a bit of fresh air, we may have killed him. We didn't care, though, nothing could touch this mood. It was a high I had never experienced. We were broken all the way down, but here we were instantly back on top. What a rush. What a high. What a great feeling. Drugs or alcohol didn't exist. We were in survival mode and appreciated every little thing. Just to be in a vehicle was a gift from God.

Germ looked over with a giant smile and started shaking my arm. "We did it, we did it, we did it! It's all over, Chad. We survived!"

Full of relief, my eyes rolled back in my head as I smiled. "Yeah, Germ... It's over." It felt better than anything. We were exhausted and I let my head rest against the seat.

The warm cloth felt euphoric and I was content to stay there for days. Two hours later, I woke to the bumping and shaking of the familiar Dub road. Germ slapped my shoulder. "Wake up, Chazz, we're here." Through my sticky, cloudy vision, I looked to the right and saw the dining hall. Ohhhh, it had been so long and it looked so beautiful. The Suburban came to a stop in front of the equipment shed and we jumped out. A shower was only minutes away. A shower! What's that?

Behind me I heard someone clapping. It was Carsten and he was heading straight for us. Across his face was the biggest smile I had ever seen. "You did it, guys, congratulations! What an accomplishment." He reached out to give each of us a congratulatory hug. We were so happy, and to see Carsten's face was an instant reminder we were back. Was I really happy to be back at the facility? I mean, I hate this place. Well, I did hate this place, but now I was OK with it. I was all about being sober and soaking in everyday natural highs. I had to do things to create those highs. Like old-fashioned hard work. Not a drug or a drink.

Even Bill was smiling, but he instructed, "Come on, jokers, unload the equipment." Anticipating a hot shower, we immediately hauled the gear into the shed, dropped it on the cold cement floor, and sprang toward the door. Andy stood in the wooden doorframe, blocking the exit. "All right, take a seat."

What! Take a seat? No! Take a shower! Come on. Everyone's face held a look of complete disappointment. Germ had to protest. "Andy, come on, please, we just want a shower."

Andy looked pissed. "Open the gear and get everything out now." There was no arguing so we reluctantly pulled out the gear. It was just another mental challenge, and it was good for us. The more times we were forced to do something good for us, the stronger we became. That's what we needed—the ability to endure pain and do the right thing, not the easiest. Our old ways chose the path of ease by escaping through drugs or alcohol. We never did what was best for the long run. We just wanted to feel better. We just wanted to get out of our own skin.

Hours felt like they had passed as we continued to hang the gear. Realistically, it was only twenty minutes or so, but with a shower that close every minute felt like hours. Finally, everything was hung and we waited for Andy's approval. *Come on, man! Please just let us take a shower.* He seemed to enjoy watching us squirm and he took his sweet time looking over all the gear. What a jerk! Patience was not my virtue. I mean, you can't blame me after not showering for sixteen days and then right when I thought I was going to shower, I was denied. I might as well have been standing under the shower head and the water not come on. Another five minutes passed as he smirked while checking and checking and checking. He never looked at us, just prowled around. I couldn't block this out. I had to wallow in the misery of waiting and waiting and waiting.

He never looked up, he calmly said, "Get out of here." WOOO HOOOO. Excitement stormed through us and we barreled out of the shed. Like a bunch of jumping beans, we shouted and cheered all the way to our separate cabins. "SHOWER TIME, SHOWER TIME, SHOWER TIME." I skipped up the steps, threw back the screen door and stormed toward the shower.

As I peeled off the underwear like a band aid, the cabin air felt foreign against my bare body. The smell emitting from my skin looked green. I stepped into the square shower box and warmed up the water. *Here we go!* I took a deep breath to truly soak in the moment and shoved my head under the water. *OHHHHHH WOWWWWWW! OH MY GOSH. OHHHHH! AMAZING! EUPHORIC!! UNBELIEVEABLE!!!* Warm water covered my head, ran down my back and dripped over my legs. It tingled, it tickled, and it was pure pleasure. Closing my eyes, I gave a giant sigh and leaned against the wall. *It's all over... Completely done... I did it. I conquered a mountain.* And I had every right to be proud of myself.

The soap, the water, the hygiene... It was by far the best feeling my body had ever experienced. No drug or drink could ever give me the pure euphoric natural feeling that shower gave me. I soaked in every moment, making sure I was completely clean, like I washed away the guilt and shame of the last four years. I washed my body over five times. It didn't seem like one or two washes were enough to eliminate the build-up of funk from not showering for that long.

With the beige towel wrapped around my waist, I crossed through the cabin and over to the only bare mattress. Fresh sheets were folded on the end and I quickly made the bed. Here came another moment. After another deep breath and a giant sigh, I snuggled deep into the warm cozy bunk. A smile so big I thought my face would crack streaked across my face. Relief, relief, and more relief washed over me. Nothing else mattered. Nothing could bother me. I didn't care. I was clean and lying in a bed with warm air filling the room.

My body kept tingling with warmth and cleanliness and comfort. Only a couple minutes passed before I slipped off into a peaceful dream. As I slept, there was probably a giant smile still stuck on my face.

SLAM! The noise of the screen door jarred me from the deep sleep. My eyes tried to open but the deep sleep delayed the process. Voices I had never heard were chatting away as the heavy thuds of work boots stomped by. Eventually my eyes focused, but my contacts were out. I couldn't make out who it was. Not that I cared, I just wanted to go back to sleep. But more guys stomped in. Realizing there was no chance of getting back to sleep, I stood from the bed and crossed the room. I didn't recognize a single person. *What's going on? Who are these kids?* Then someone spoke, "Hey, you just got back from the Trip, didn't you?"

Suddenly I felt proud and strong and said, "Yeah man, just a couple hours ago." His eyes filled with wonder and he looked at me like I had something he desperately needed. Like a cup of water when you're stranded in the desert. He was a newbie. All these clowns were, it was as clear as day. But that's how this place works. You come in a complete joker and you walk out a man. I had passed through a sacred ritual. I had what everyone else wanted. I was on top. I had seniority. I had conquered the Trip.

Over the next nine days, the other Trip guys and I took control of the place. We were the example and we had all the right advice. We were just as good as the counselors. In every one of the new guys, we saw ourselves and knew exactly what they needed to hear. Just the thought of the newbies having no idea of what was coming made us chuckle. No one escapes any process of the facility, and no one escapes the power of Family Week and the Trip. You can't. It would be like saying you come out the same person as when you went into war. Things change you whether you want them to or not. Each and every one of us came out a man and we were ready to face life. The

Trip, Family Week, the work days, the group sessions, the meetings, the environment had all done us justice. It was like black and white. Day and night.

Over the next nine days, Chris, Bran, Germ, Ken, David, and Thomas left for their halfway houses. They were like my brothers, and we shared something that we will never share with any other person. We had been through a battle together and we were still standing.

When my day came, I packed my bags, went through a small graduating ceremony, and jumped into the same vehicle that brought me there. My mind flooded with endorphins. I did it. I survived. And now I was leaving...

Epilogue

After the two months at the Wilderness Treatment Center, I headed to the halfway house in Minnesota. Sure, it was not what I wanted to do but I was going with the flow, something I had never done before. The halfway house was by no means luxurious or even average. It was a bit run down, but at the time it seemed great. I had just come out of the woods, so anything that produced heat and running water sounded fantastic. During my stay, I attended a local high school where I finished my three remaining core classes. The school had a separate program built for people who were attending halfway houses or other programs. This way the students could go to school and live a healthy life. It was truly a remarkable program for the school to conduct, and I commend them for their efforts. There was no teaching, but instead we worked different packets that taught the material to us. It was actually nice. No teachers. No extracurricular nonsense. Just get the work done and you pass the course. Of course everything was graded, but it was not terribly hard.

After school I went straight to work at a local pizza place. Everything was great. I was doing school, I was working, and I was staying sober. Nonetheless, I was ready to come home. A month and a half later, I completed the three courses and saw no reason to remain at the halfway house. Some of the residents were relapsing, and I felt the environment was no longer suitable for my needs. My parents agreed, and despite the counselors' best attempts to keep me there my parents brought me home, but with very strict conditions. I would have agreed to anything, just as long as they brought me home. They required me to attend recovery meetings, take random drug tests, and continue working the program. However, they did give me the freedom that I deserved, and as long as I didn't mess up, they were willing to work with me. Our relationship was mended.

It was near the end of April of 2004 when my brother and mom picked me up from the airport. Other than my family, I had not told another soul about my return. I wanted to surprise everyone. It was fun and exciting to show up at places where I knew my friends were hanging out.

Over the next seven months, I stayed sober and worked at a local sub shop. Sobriety was not an issue. During July, I received a letter of congratulations on being accepted to a university in Georgia. Upon completing my three core courses in Minnesota, the high school I had attended since the fourth grade awarded me my diploma. What a blessing! Now I was going off to college. I was sober and starting fresh. A new life, a second chance, and it was all owed to my parents. Thank you.

Reflection

Throughout the book, I touched on the reasons I developed a pattern of using drugs and alcohol. Reasons like anxiety, need for acceptance, peer pressure, depression, impulsiveness, and identity confusion all came together to create one giant monster: addiction. But where was the true beginning? Where did these feelings and thoughts come from? What was the main source?

Any individual who consistently abuses drugs or alcohol is experiencing some or many serious negative consequences. Just to name a few: jail, arrests, hangovers, poor work performance, poor school performance, health problems, financial problems... the list goes on. So why would anyone who experiences so many hardships keep going back to the same thing that is causing the problems? It doesn't make sense. It's literally insane!

Well, based on personal experience, individuals who constantly abuse drugs and alcohol are receiving some form of positive reinforcement that is so strong it outweighs all the other negative consequences. But what could possibly be so strong that it feels better than a giant compounding list of negative consequences? Well, let's look at it this way: is it something that feels so good or is there really something that hurts so bad that to not feel it feels so good... Hmm?

What could possibly hurt so bad that it feels so good to not feel it? Easy...pain. Pain is the answer. But what causes the pain? Well, it could be a number of things, but for me and many alcoholics, it is a feeling of insecurity. In addict terms, it's a feeling that your own skin is your enemy. Whether you realize it or not, just being yourself is the worst pain you could ever experience. But where does that feeling of insecurity come from? Are addicts and alcoholics born with it or did it develop from interacting with society?

I don't believe we were born with it, but I do believe we were all born with different talents. By having a particular talent, other areas may seem like weak spots when comparing oneself to society. As far as the weak spots go, it's not a matter of nature versus nurture, but instead nature multiplied by nurture. The weak spots or even talents are what can be increased or decreased by nurture. Nurture can be defined as interactions with society, caregivers, or both. But society is the true culprit. Society comes in and emphasizes those weak spots to a level that creates an unbearable pain. Let me explain by tracing the beginning of my insecurities all the way back to adolescence. Before I begin, let me emphasize what I am about to explain is just a piece of the big puzzle, not the true source.

Adolescence and identity confusion go hand-in-hand, and it's common and normal for adolescents to experience identity confusion. In fact, it's healthy. Adolescence is a period in one's life where he or she tries to figure out who he or she is. The beginning process for identity searching is probably the hardest. Sure, parents, society, media, friends have all offered different paths, but the reality is there are many options. Adolescence is a time to try out different options. For example, one might join a sports team, an acting club, a debate team, a social group, a gothic clique, a band, or whatever. You get the point. The fact of the matter is if they are not comfortable in whatever group they join, an anxious feeling will be created.

The first group I joined was the basketball team. Sports were the one group I truly knew. During childhood, I played baseball, soccer, and basketball. In these leagues I was a star. I always started and always played the entire game. It was a comforting feeling and my confidence levels soared.

However, upon entering the seventh grade everything changed. The seventh grade basketball team was the beginning of a steep downfall. Looking back, I wish I would have never made the team, but I was good and that's all I knew, sports. Sports were my identity. Unfortunately, the school team, naturally being very competitive, only looked to play and grow those athletes who were the best. I was good, but not one of the top five. Doomed from the beginning, I hardly worked with the coaches. During the first game, I didn't play a single minute and it absolutely crushed me. My world came crashing down. It just didn't make sense that I would go from playing every second to not playing a single second. I was a star. I helped the team. What happened? How could I go from the star to the bench? I didn't understand. It hurt at an unbearable level. This is where sports can go so wrong. People focus only on winning and that comes with a price. The price is others who must lose. Sure some win, but think about how many lose.

In my eyes, I went from being a star player to a star loser. My self-esteem plummeted. Every day at practice or school I felt insecure, worried, and scared of the next comment about not being good enough. Anxiety was inevitable. Having sports as my life and then having disappointment thrown in my face completely ruined my self-esteem. My power, my source, my confidence had been crushed. Without confidence I could never be who I was really meant to be. I mean, if you don't believe in yourself, you have nothing. I had nothing. Without confidence in myself, everything else suffered.

Throughout seventh and eighth grades, I battled and battled and battled to gain confidence the best way I knew possible, sports. Every day, I stayed determined to get better, and would practice for hours. Seventh grade summer was spent trying to shoot thirty thousand baskets on top of team practice and summer camps. It helped and I played a little more, but I was never one of the starting five players. No amount of practice was enough to make me that star again. Despite the hours, days, weeks of practice, failure remained my best friend. The weed of anxiety, born from insecurity, grew to a new height. I dreaded going to school.

So here I was, depressed, anxious, and empty on self-esteem. It was the summer before ninth grade and I was desperate for a change. Anything to relieve this feeling of failure, depression, and anxiety.

The first time I held a miniature bottle containing an alcoholic liquid I was excited for something different. The warm tingling sensation went flowing down my throat. Another bottle down and fifteen minutes later, I felt different. Not in my skin. No depression, no anxiety, no failure, and no zero self-esteem. It was perfect. All those negative feelings were gone! It felt great. A few weeks later I tried weed. It helped even more. Even better, I didn't get hangovers and I could do it whenever and more discreetly.

All it took was one try and the rest is history. One hit, one drink, one feeling of impairment. My brain clicked into addiction, it dialed in, and with the final turn, the locking bolt popped and I stepped into a world of comfort. It was so beautiful, so appealing, and the warm light was shining brightly. It was paradise not living in feelings of depression, anxiety, failure, and insecurity. The room felt like a world full of mystical rivers, enchanted animals, luscious greens, and sparkling blues. The feeling was of pure beauty. How could I resist? I couldn't. It was too comforting. Really, deep down, that's all I wanted—comfort! Comfort, for me, meant peace and security with myself. Up until the first feeling of impairment, my whole life was engulfed in insecurity. Now it was all gone.

Now, I do believe I have a weak spot that's susceptible to ridicule; however, I believe that weak spot was created from a talent I was given. The talent is having a huge heart that cares about other people and how other people are feeling. But with a caring heart comes the side effect of being hypersensitive to other people's comments, creating my weak spot. It's not that we were necessarily born with weak spots, but instead they are simply just a side effect of our talents. All my life I have been sensitive to any comment that picked at me, and these comments caused tremendous amounts of pain and insecurity even though on the surface level they didn't seem like that big of a deal. But when the pain was there, the offering of substances came with promises of a life without pain.

Pain had been building and building throughout junior high. Eventually it became so bad that I was desperate for relief. Unfortunately the devil knew just that, so he came skipping along with a bottle of rum in one hand and a joint in the other. The devil knew he could derail me by offering his sweetest deal. The devil wanted me out of the way. Out of the way meant not on God's side. Not on God's side meant I would not be able to use my God-given talents to aid in the battle of good and evil. The devil knows I have the potential to do great, remarkable things. Each of us has a great potential. This is exactly what the devil doesn't want. He knows that God already has enough power on his side, and the last thing the devil needs is another person on God's side. Why else would there be constant temptations to engage in self-destructive behaviors? Why else would there be influences pulling you back toward the righteous side? It's a game of tug of war and humans are the flag dangling from the middle. In the end, we are the ones who make the decision to allow ourselves to be pulled to one side or the other.

But why is the pull toward the evil side so much more appealing for some? Well, God is the creator and God has the power. The devil needs as much help as he can get if he wants to win. So how does the devil get us away from God? He goes for the weak spots. He goes for the areas he knows you can hardly resist. If you have pain, he offers a sweet, easy, path of comfort. For me, this is substances.

I had no problem signing up for that program. I jumped into the room with no hesitation and it felt so good. But it was a deception, a lie, an empty promise. After stepping into the room, the door slams behind you. The radiating light extinguishes. It's pitch black. The humming lullaby turns into sardonic laughter. The tingling sensation turns into fingers that are grasping, holding, and never letting go. You try to reach back, but the door—it's gone! No handle, no frame, just cold, damp, concrete walls. You panic because you're lost. You don't know what to do. So you chase that feeling of comfort. You chase that security. You chase that high. But you're not getting anywhere.

The fingers of addiction hold tight, but still that comforting feeling you're chasing is so close. In fact, it's dangling right in front of you, tempting you, just reach and you'll grab it. So you stretch and stretch and stretch. You use and use and use, but you never grasp a true comforting feeling. You think the feeling you want is there, inches away. If you just try harder... If you just use more, you can be at peace. You're sure of this, so you keep trying, you keep using. This time your fingers touch it and you can feel the comfort. It tingles and you remember how good it felt. You can't feel a true comforting feeling, but it keeps you motivated. Your desire is to be at peace, to be at peace with yourself. You want to be submerged in comfort. Just use more and you will feel comfort.

Now you're determined. You have to feel comfort. You have to have something that takes away the pain, you have to have something to get out of your own skin, so you pour forth all efforts. Nothing else matters, not school, not family, not your spouse, not your kids, not your job, nothing. Not even the negative consequences matter, just a need for comfort. So you keep using, you keep trying to comfort yourself. You keep trying to not feel your own skin. By now you're losing so much. All the things that used to make you happy are slowly disappearing. Even worse, the negative consequences are burying you. Now in a desperate state to gain comfort, you use more and everything else gets pushed aside.

Because at one point alcohol and drugs did equal comfort, you keep trying, you keep using. So you reach again, you miss again and you reach again. You keep using drugs and alcohol, but that comfort is never fully achieved, that comfort is never constant. However, your brain only remembers the first high. Back when you hadn't lost anything to drugs or alcohol, back when you didn't experience negative consequences, back when you only got comfort, back when you stepped into that room.

The healthy relationships are losing patience. They're being neglected. But whatever. You have to grab and hold comfort first. Once you grab it, then you'll give your full attention to the relationships. The comfort must come first. It's still right there. Just reach. Just take a drink. Just take a pill. Just take a hit. Just snort a line. Just shoot a needle. Just reach... This time everything will be better.

No, it won't! It will never be better. It will never be different. It will never change. You will always be reaching, always missing, always trying, always tired, always disappointed and always in pain. The worst part is that the pain gets worse.

But there is an answer. One answer, one option, one path to cure this cycle. The one answer you don't want to hear. The one answer that makes you cover your ears whenever you even think it's being mentioned. The single answer that makes you cringe.

TURN AROUND! Completely around! You have to admit and accept you have a problem. Then you can turn to the help of the ones that love you.

Behind you in the damp concrete wall a light is shining. It's in a shape resembling a door. No way! You looked back earlier and it was gone. Why? Because you were still facing forward. You were still using. The door is only offered when you're facing it, not looking over your shoulder. Only when you're not using can you see the light, the light being the help of others.

So there's the seam, but where is the handle? Well, it's not that easy. Now you have to face what you've neglected. You have to own up to your selfishness. You actually have to take responsibility. You must make amends where possible. But it's so hard! It's so hard to say, "I'm sorry." Besides, they've heard that before. They won't buy it. Only through actions and consistent behavior will the neglected believe you. Words are the first part, but words are like a stalk of the plant and the plant needs roots to deliver the nutrients. The roots are consistent behavior and with time, the neglected will believe. They want you to succeed and they want to show their love. Besides, they have always loved you. Even when you were out being a jerk. Trust me, if they didn't love you, they would have completely written you off. The only reason the love might be low is because you've consistently pushed them away by focusing on that comfort. It's not your fault—but it is. To them it is. They don't get it, they don't understand, and in fact, they will probably never understand. But it's OK. As long as you show steady behavior, that door handle will form and you can pull it open.

You can step back into the world with light, the world without empty promises. After being in the dark for so long, the light is too bright. It makes you squint and shudder. It burns, it hurts, it's painful, and it shows your true colors. It shows what a piece of crap you have been. Immediately shame and guilt take control. All your wounds are out in the open, your flaws, your weak spots—and everyone can see them. The darkness seems so much safer. At least in the dark you don't have to see your flaws and mistakes. Not to mention the dangling comfort is tapping you on the shoulder. It's there. Within reach! No way! You can actually grab it.

And so you do. You take that hit, that drink, that needle, that line and you fall back into the room. Back in the darkness. But for a moment you can hold the comfort. Embrace the comfort. Love the comfort. Love the drug. But before you know it, it's gone. Back to reaching. The door slams shut, separating you from the neglected. It's colder this time. Remembering the warmth of the light makes the room seem that much colder. You remember the warmth of your loved ones, but that light, it was too much, too much negative attention, and so you do what you know best. You start using again. Reaching again. Still missing and missing. Using. Drinking. Drugging. Eventually you get tired and turn around. You accept help, you make apologies, and you demonstrate consistent behavior. The handle appears and you open the door, stepping back into the light. This time you know what to expect, but that doesn't matter. The light burns, it hurts and the flaws are still there. The shame and guilt are overwhelming. Comfort pokes your shoulder. You resist! You remember the pain. You remember the cold, the dark, the loneliness. The comforting poking can't bother you this time. The pain was too much and memories of pain keep you strong.

But before you know it you start to forget the pain. It fades. You're living sober. You've got this. You'll never go back to that. It's a good thought, but only a thought, not a feeling. The actual pain has been snuffed by time. It's natural, a defense mechanism. Your mind can't wallow in pain forever. But the pain was the only thing restraining the comfort to a poke. Now comfort is grabbing. Grabbing your shoulder, trying to pull you in, trying everything it can, offering its best deal. Sign now and get a five hundred dollar credit. No? OK, how about five years free. Come on. We'll be friends again. I'm sorry. I won't do it again. You can hold me all you want. Just a drink, just a hit, just a line, just a shot. Come on, man, we're pals, remember? "Here, dude, you want a free hit? I'll buy your drinks." It's funny, every time I quit I heard statements just like that. But when I was using, no one ever offered anything for free.

A crucial decision lies before you. What to do? What to do? You look back at the dangling comfort. Then forward. Then back. The debate is strong. If you've only been relying on remembering the pain, then it's all over. The call is too strong. Something has to be in front of you, something different from pain, something stronger, something that for me gives me a different high. My brain has been programmed to enjoy a high, which is also natural. Endorphins are released through plenty of healthy things: love, exercise, achievement, peace, even petting a dog. It's all proven. Highs are good. The current world has just made it easier to get them with substances. But the easy route comes with side effects. Serious side effects. Side effects so bad that you do whatever it takes to get rid of them. So you continue on the path that offered the fake high. The side effects spoil everything however. It's like a piece of fecal matter floating in an alcoholic beverage. Sure you're getting drunk, but you're also getting sick. Sick in the body, sick in the mind, and sick in your soul.

Only through natural highs do you avoid the side effects. Exercising, loving, petting a dog, going for a hike, watching the sunrise, achieving—it doesn't matter what you do, but you have to find something that gives you a natural high. It may not be as easy, it may not be instant, but through persistence a natural high is possible. Once you find what works, you have to embrace it. Give your best effort. Do what makes you feel good even when you don't really feel like it. Once that natural high is there, soak it in. Cherish it. Love it. Never let go. It's OK. It's clean. It's pure. There is no floating fecal matter, just a cold, clean, glass of water. The water may not tingle, but you won't be sick. You will be living.

Never forget about the addiction, though. It's not going anywhere just because you think you've found what works to keep you sober. The second you think you've got it conquered is the second you're doomed. Back to the dark room and this time you may not get out. You have to consciously remind yourself that the addiction is still there, just over your shoulder and still dangling dangerously within reach. Whether this means going to meetings, taking time to remember, or whatever, you must turn your back on it and ignore it. Addiction is patient and will never turn its back on you. It's your best friend. Like a loyal dog, it will wait patiently no matter what. Just waiting and whimpering. Block it out, but know it's there. It may be whimpering, but it has other intentions. Intentions to bite. Intentions to kill. Intentions to sink its teeth deep into your soul.

14662669R10118

Made in the USA
Lexington, KY
12 April 2012